Preaching and Teaching the Gospels to Children

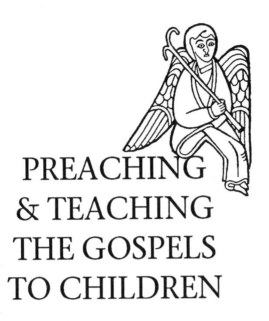

PREACHING
& TEACHING
THE GOSPELS
TO CHILDREN

Sean McEntee

THE COLUMBA PRESS
DUBLIN 1992

First edition, 1992, published by
THE COLUMBA PRESS
93 The Rise, Mount Merrion, Blackrock, Co Dublin

Cover by Bill Bolger
Origination by The Columba Press
Printed in the United States of America

ISBN 1 85607 052 2

Contents

Introduction

When we are planning homilies for children we have to think like teachers. Teachers think very purposefully. A lesson in the classroom has a beginning, a middle and an end that is dictated by insights from psychology, sociology and education.

A teacher's lesson plan is, first of all, guided by an overall learning objective. A theme or topic to be learned goes through the steps of:
(a) being introduced,
(b) being explored and enlarged, and
(c) being reinforced through learning activities.

These steps come from a larger learning theory which proposes principles that preachers have to bear in mind.

Children think concretely.

Children learn out of their own range of limited life-experiences.

Children work out of a strong sense of feeling (which is supported as they grow older by an equally strong intellectual activity).

Children learn through activity (a teacher provides appropriate learning opportunities and activities for children).

I have followed a teaching style and process in preparing this book for preachers. Here are the steps I follow for each Sunday:

	Overview
Step One	Focusing Experiences
Step Two	Exploring the Word of God
Step Three	Call to Faith
Step Four	Call to action

Overview

In the Overview for each Sunday, the key issues of the gospel are outlined and clarified, perhaps, by adding some biblical or liturgical background. From this adult perspective the preacher is encouraged to move down a gear into the cultural, emotional, linguistic, and experiential world of children to accommodate children's insights, experiences, and ways of learning. The challenge presented to children will then be seen to have devolved from a larger picture and not be in any way arbitrary, artificial, or free-floating.

The overview is the device we use for alerting preachers to the overall thrust of the gospel and then to suggest an approach that seems to meet the needs of children.

Step One: Focusing Experiences

By focusing on appropriate experiences from the child's world, we are creating emotional and experiential access routes for the gospel message. We are creating a friendly environment, a friendly atmosphere for the gospel. We are creating a receptivity in the child's mind, a row of antennae that are tuned in to what the gospel will be saying.

These are called focusing experiences because they focus the child's attention, interest and feeling on the issues which the gospel will address.

Step Two: Exploring the Word of God

Here we explore and enlarge. The gospel story is the vital element. We cannot presume that the story has been heard in the course of the formal reading. We have to tell it again, this time adding our own style, our own nuances, our own phrases, our enlargements of character, our refinements of feelings, our local colouring. Now each one of us is a story-teller to the children. The gospel proclaimed a few moments previously needs more work, needs to be enlarged a little, needs to be spoken differently, needs to be delivered differently, supported by words children use, by gestures and inflexions children understand.

The gospel story is full of richness. Full of colour. Full of power. We have to dance and weave a little with the story. Warm to the story. Get into it. Make it our own. Our own personal echoes and style have to reverberate through the story. We are all story-tellers at heart. Given the right audience we delight in telling stories. Our opportunity to tantalise!

We should not sideline the gospel story to deliver moral or doctrinal points. The story should not be disposed of in a few summary sentences. This tendency to use the gospel story as a quarry for points came from the days when preachers felt the need to give points of doctrine a constant airing. An apologetical approach had precedence over a scriptural approach! The story was not given a chance to interact with imagination! The gospel stories do not tire easily but they must be told in a way that strokes the imagination. And children are all feeling and imagination!

Stories work their own magic, have a life of their own and leave their own traces. The biblical stories and anecdotes continue to rattle around inside us and reappear at odd moments. The wonderful thing about a story is that it grows with us. It challenges us as we are, at whatever level of experience we're at.

We must not avoid gospel stories about death, hell, sheep and goats, damnation and the gnashing of teeth. These judgement stories are not news items, mathematical details or historical descriptions to frighten the children but stories to inhabit their imagination, to help their reflection, to help their search for wisdom. They will find a way to accommodate a God of love with a God of judgement.

In this book the gospel story forms the heart of the homily. Many of the stories are retold in a familiar way to hint at a style the homilist might follow.

You may decide to use a questions technique, in a dialogue homily situation, to interact with the listening/learning group. It is suggested that questions should follow a pattern, starting first with factual questions, then following with feeling and insight questions.

Step Three: Call to Faith

We need to enunciate, as simply and directly as possible, the call of the readings. In this book, the call is a one-paragraph speech linked to the focusing, telling and exploration that went before. It is a natural highpoint in which the threads are all pulled together. It is a moment of vision, challenge and appeal. In this moment we make the Word of God active for the children.

Step Four: Call to Action

The Call to Action clarifies and underlines the Call to Faith. We organise actions that reinforce what we have agreed is the call and challenge of this gospel. The actions suggested must be practical and possible for children. The purpose of these actions is to suggest the intimate connection between liturgy and life, between hearing the Word and doing the Word. It is an important part of the whole process. As teachers always say, doing is vital to learning! I have suggested some actions that seem to have worked well. You will need, of course, to adapt and supplement these to suit your own particular circumstances.

A Last Word

Teachers sometimes do not start at the beginning. In this book the steps of the learning process are interchangeable. We may start, on occasions, not with the Focusing Experiences but with the Call to Action and follow with the Exploration of the Word. We are at liberty to work either backwards or forwards through the steps. Remember, however, that fidelity to the key idea proposed in the Overview is essential. The process is flexible within that limitation.

First Sunday of Advent

Gospel

A reading from the holy Gospel according to Matthew (24:37-44)

Be on your guard, then, because you do not know what day your Lord will come. If the owner of a house knew the time when the thief would come, you can be sure that he would stay awake and not let the thief break into his house. So then, you also must always be ready, because the Son of Man will come at an hour when you are not expecting him.

This is the Gospel of the Lord.

Overview

Children like the idea of preparation. They like the planning, the action and savouring the event to be celebrated. There can be as much excitement in the preparation as in the event itself. Advent can appeal to them.

It's Advent! We need to get down to the business of talking to God, listening to God, building up our friendship with God! Otherwise we could miss out on a chance to be in good shape for Christmas and the coming of God's Son!

Focusing Experiences

Explore all the many and varied things we do to get ready for holidays, for the return to school, for a school concert, for a competition, for a sporting event, for the arrival of a celebrity.

What do we mean by being properly prepared? – putting thought and effort into preparation, listening, speaking, training, practising, repeating, learning.

Exploring the Word of God

In the days before Jesus the most talked-about hero of the time was God's Messiah. Everyone wanted to meet the Messiah. Everyone wanted to live long enough to be around when the Messiah came. Everyone wanted to be friends with the Messiah. Everyone was expecting the Messiah, but yet, at the same time, not exactly sure what to look for or expect. Jesus spoke like one who knew. Jesus spoke like one who knew God's plans for the Messiah. He told the people to prepare for the Messiah, to stay on the watch, to keep up their wait. Things were about to happen. The time was near. Very close. He said that the quality of the waiting and watching and listening had to be a hundred per cent. Jesus told them they'd have to watch and wait with the sharpness and the alertness of a person tipped off about the time a burglar would try to break into their house.

Call to Faith

Jesus invites us to prepare. Jesus invites us to listen. He wants us to grow more into God's people. You heard what he said in today's gospel: Prepare! Be on your guard! Watch! You are called to prepare for Christmas. You are called to prepare for Christmas by listening to God, talking to God and letting God more into your life.

Call to Action

Let's prepare a welcome for Jesus by making an Advent wreath.
Sing songs of praise to God for Jesus.
At a quiet time, consider virtues that need to be practised in preparation for Christmas.
At a quiet time, consider faults that need to be corrected.
Make banners with the slogans: Prepare! Be ready!

Second Sunday of Advent

Gospel

A reading from the holy Gospel according to Matthew (3:1-12)
At that time John the Baptist came to the desert of Judaea and started preaching: 'Turn away from your sins,' he said, 'because the Kingdom of heaven is near!' John was the man the prophet Isaiah was talking about when he said,
'Someone is shouting in the desert,
"Prepare a road for the Lord;
Make straight a path for him to travel!"'
John's clothes were made of camel's hair; he wore a leather belt round his waist and his food was locusts and wild honey. People came to him from Jerusalem, from the whole province of Judaea and from all the country near the river Jordan. They confessed their sins and he baptised them in the Jordan.
This is the Gospel of the Lord.

Overview

X John the Baptist was sent by God to announce to God's people the coming of the Messiah. John the Baptist told the people how they had to prepare. He told them to let goodness shine out in their lives. He told them to change their ways. He told them to prepare for the new world that the Messiah would bring. X

Children enjoy exploring John the Baptist's character. They all aspire to experience, in play, the freedom John the Baptist expressed through the makeshift clothes he wore and the primitive food he ate. John the Baptist is a prophet they like.

Focusing Experiences

Know any John the Baptist types – prophets, gurus, hermits, monks, civil/human rights activists, preachers, missionaries, feminists? Anyone promoting a cause or a mission that they really want to persuade people about?

Exploring the Word of God

John the Baptist was a kind of explorer, guru, old-style preacher. His message about the Messiah burned inside him. He had thoughts only for that message. No time for well-cut clothes or juicy food. What people in high places thought of him didn't bother him in the slightest. His thoughts were about God. How could he get people to hear his message? How could he get people to change their ways and become more and more God's people? That's what bothered him. That was his agenda. That was his programme. That's where he wanted the action.

In the days of Jesus any news of the Messiah was sure to get people excited, and John the Baptist now had news of the Messiah that would really cause a stir. John announced that the the Messiah was among them!

John was regarded by the people as one of God's prophets and any-thing he said was listened to with attention. His news of the Messiah brought them crowding around him for more details, for directions, for advice. He was causing a tremendous buzz among the people.

Call to Faith
We are called to listen to John the Baptist. We are called to heed his words announcing Jesus to the world. We are called to make Jesus wel-come. We are invited, in the time up to Christmas, to become more and more God's people. We are invited to prepare to give Jesus a marvellous welcome at Christmas time.

Call to Action
Write about John the Baptist.
Write interview questions for John the Baptist about his feelings, his concerns, his message.
Continue the preparation of welcome for Christmas.
Honour/welcome Jesus with songs and hymns of praise.
Continue to display the Advent wreath.

Third Sunday of Advent

Gospel

A reading from the holy Gospel according to Matthew (11:2-11)

When John the Baptist heard in prison about the things that Christ was doing, he sent some of his disciples to him. 'Tell us,' they asked Jesus, 'are you the one John said was going to come, or should we expect someone else?'

Jesus answered, 'Go back and tell John what you are hearing and seeing: the blind can see, the lame can walk, those who suffer from dreaded skin-diseases are made clean, the deaf hear, the dead are brought back to life, and the Good News is preached to the poor.'

This is the Gospel of the Lord.

Overview

The Bible said the Messiah would heal the sick. The disciples of John the Baptist could see for themselves that Jesus was healing the sick. This evidence confirmed for John the Baptist that Jesus was the Messiah.

Children know what it is to have confidence in their teacher, their priest, their parents. John had confidence in Jesus. Jesus was the real thing for John. Jesus was the Messiah.

Focusing Experiences

You know about believing in someone, and having your belief in someone confirmed by their actions. It's nice to have confidence in someone you care about.

You like to have confidence in brothers and sisters.

You like to feel they will be there for you when you need them. When they support you in something or other you are doing, your confidence in them is strengthened. You are more convinced than ever they are on your side.

You like to have confidence in parents, like to feel they love you, like to feel you're important to them. You may even ask them if they love you. You like to be sure. When they do something to give you encouragement or take time out with you, it makes you feel loved. It makes you feel more sure about their love. Your confidence in them grows.

You like to have confidence in your teachers.

You like to have confidence in your priest.

Exploring the Word of God

John the Baptist was arrested and imprisoned for speaking out against the king. He said the king should not have divorced his wife.

John's only thoughts in prison were about the Messiah. He heard the stories that Jesus was curing the sick. And John knew only too well that the Bible said the Messiah would be known by his cures and miracles. John sent some of his disciples to Jesus to ask him directly if he was the Messiah. Jesus told them to look around them at the evidence. They went back to John to say that Jesus was doing what the Bible said the Messiah would do. John's deep belief in Jesus was confirmed. His confidence in Jesus was enhanced, enriched, deepened, strengthened.

Call to Faith
We are called to share John's faith in Jesus. We are called to have heart in Jesus. We are called to have confidence in Jesus. We are called to see Jesus as God's Messiah among us.

Call to Action
To express our confidence in Jesus we are going to sing and praise his name, sing a song that expresses our belief in Jesus.
Let's make out a pattern of prayer sentences that expresses our belief in Jesus:
Jesus, we love you.
Jesus, we believe in you.
Jesus, we are with you.
Jesus, we follow you wherever you go.
Saint Patrick's breastplate is a speech and a prayer of confidence in Jesus. Look it up and print it out on a decorated scroll.

Fourth Sunday of Advent

Gospel

A reading from the holy Gospel according to Matthew (1: 18-24)

This is how the birth of Jesus Christ took place. His mother Mary was engaged to Joseph, but before they were married, she found out that she was going to have a baby by the Holy Spirit. Joseph was a man who always did what was right, but he did not want to disgrace Mary publicly; so he made plans to break the engagement privately. While he was thinking about this, an angel of the Lord appeared to him in a dream and said, 'Joseph, descendant of David, do not be afraid to take Mary to be your wife. For it is by the Holy Spirit that she has conceived. She will have a son, and you will name him Jesus – because he will save his people from their sins.'

Now all this happened in order to make what the Lord had said through the prophet come true, 'A virgin will become pregnant and have a son, and he will be called Immanuel' (which means, 'God is with us').

So when Joseph woke up, he married Mary, as the angel of the Lord had told him to do.

This is the Gospel of the Lord.

Overview

Joseph was confused by the news that Mary was going to have a baby. He thought about leaving her. Mary was confused by the news that she was going to be the mother of God's Son. She thought that perhaps she wasn't up to it. But they both had this super confidence in God. And they let God take a hand in resolving their confusion.

Conception, pregnacy and worried fathers is not an area preachers to children feel comfortable with. But this pre-Christmas story can be told with delicacy and in a way that leaves the children with affection for Joseph and Mary.

Focusing Experiences

People get confused about things. You are asked to do something at home and you're not sure if it's a punishment or a compliment. But you get it sorted out. You talk it out.

At school you are asked to do a task and you are worried because you might get it wrong. But the teacher encourages you and gives you confidence and you get on with it and it works out alright.

The priest talks about sin and you're not sure sure if you should feel bad about what you've done. But you think about it and sure you should feel bad about what you've done, but at the same time you know God loves you and wants you to feel good with yourself and with others.

Exploring the Word of God

Joseph and Mary were religious people. They took their guidance from God and from his holy Bible. Mary and Joseph felt confused about what they seemed to be getting into for God. It is easy to understand why Mary and Joseph were worried and unsure.

Joseph got the news that Mary was expecting a baby. He wasn't the baby's father. He was dumbfounded and shocked at the revelation that she was going to have a child. He consulted with friends and relations, and it was agreed that his engagement to Mary should be broken off. This decision filled his heart with sadness because he loved Mary.

The night before he was to break off his engagement to Mary he had a dream. It was as real as anything he had ever seen. In the dream God's angel told him not to break off his engagement, that Mary was part of God's plan to save the world. The angel told Joseph that Mary's son would be the Son of God. Indeed the glory of it all was that Mary, alone of all the women in the world, had been chosen to be the mother of God's Son, an honour never before given to any woman. Joseph was told that he, too, was part of God's plan. He was to take Mary home to be his wife. He was commissioned to love her with all his heart and guard her with all his might and strength. Joseph's depression lifted and he couldn't wait to go and share with his beloved wife Mary everything the angel had told him.

Call to Faith

We are called to applaud Mary and Joseph for listening to God, for letting God guide them and direct them to a new understanding of their problem. We applaud them for letting God take away their worries. Above all we applaud them for giving us God's Son.

We are called to welcome Jesus into the world as God's Son even if we are confused by God becoming a baby who will be born to a poor Jewish couple called Joseph and Mary.

Call to Action

We applaud Mary and Joseph by doing the following actions to-day or this week:

Sing a ballad about the story of Mary and Joseph.

Write about the problem each one of them had to face.

Write a tribute (a speech) to them.

The Nativity of Our Lord

Gospel

A reading from the holy Gospel according to Luke (2:1-14)

At that time the Emperor Augustus ordered a census to be taken throughout the Roman Empire.

Joseph went from the town of Nazareth in Galilee to the town of Bethlehem in Judaea, the birthplace of King David. Joseph went there because he was a descendant of David. He went to register with Mary, who was promised in marriage to him. She was pregnant, and while they were in Bethlehem, the time came for her to have her baby. She gave birth to her first son, wrapped him in strips of cloth and laid him in a manger – there was no room for them to stay in the inn.

There were some shepherds in that part of the country who were spending the night in the fields, taking care of their flocks. An angel of the Lord appeared to them, and the glory of the Lord shone over them. They were terribly afraid, but the angel said to them, 'Don't be afraid! I am here with good news for you, which will bring great joy to all the people. This very day in David's town, your Saviour was born – Christ the Lord! And this is what will prove it to you: you will find a baby wrapped in strips of cloth and lying in a manger.'

Suddenly a great army of heaven's angels appeared with the angel, singing praises to God: 'Glory to God in the highest heaven, and peace on earth to those with whom he is pleased!'

This is the Gospel of the Lord.

Overview

Nothing will ever be the same again. The Son of God has come among us. It is a time of joy and welcome. The waiting is over. With all our hearts we thank and praise God for giving us Jesus.

For the children it is a time of undiluted celebration. Hymns, processions and visits to the crib. Today should be seen as an opportunity to celebrate and celebrate again.

Focusing Experiences

A big event. A music celebration. A festival. A sports extravaganza. Moments of really intense excitement. A time when something quite extraordinary happens. A friend, a parent rescued from a plane crash. Someone saved from drowning. A hostage released.

Remember a special time of excitement in your life? You felt like crying. You felt like singing. You felt like dancing. You felt a bit overcome by all the action.

Exploring the Word of God

The shepherds on that hillside were religious people. They were waiting for God's Messiah, like their people before them. They often talked about it, wondered and waited.

Then the quiet night filled with this most intense excitement for them. They became aware of a new-born Saviour. The news was in the very air. They were extremely excited and afraid. Nothing like this had ever happened to them. For a while they were completely overcome by the excitement. They made their way down the hill to Bethlehem. They threw themselves on the ground before the new born baby and adored him as their Lord and Saviour.

Call to Faith

We are called to welcome the Saviour. We are called to welcome Jesus. We are called to thank God for giving us Jesus. We are called to thank God for giving us Jesus who is our Saviour Lord. We are called to celebrate with hands and feet and hearts and voices!

Call to Action

Dance with delight for Jesus.

Sing Christmas carols of welcome to Jesus.

Make a procession with covered lights to the crib, singing as you go and singing as you gather around the crib and singing as you leave.

Ask the priest to proclaim a special word of thanks to God for Jesus.

Holy Family of Jesus, Mary and Joseph

Gospel

A reading from the holy Gospel according to Matthew (2:13-15,19-23)

After they had left, an angel of the Lord appeared in a dream to Joseph and said, 'Herod will be looking for the child in order to kill him. So get up, take the child and his mother and escape to Egypt, and stay there until I tell you to leave.'

Joseph got up, took the child and his mother, and left during the night for Egypt, where he stayed until Herod died. This was done to make what the Lord had said through the prophet come true, 'I called my Son out of Egypt.'

After Herod died, an angel of the Lord appeared in a dream to Joseph in Egypt and said, 'Get up, take the child and his mother, and go back to the land of Israel, because those who tried to kill the child are dead.' So Joseph got up, took the child and his mother, and went back to Israel.

But when Joseph heard that Archelaus had succeeded his father Herod as king of Judaea, he was afraid to go there. He was given more instructions in a dream and made his home in a town named Nazareth. And so what the prophets had said came true: 'He will be called a Nazarene.'
This is the Gospel of the Lord.

Overview

Joseph, Mary and the child Jesus had to move home. Leave friends. Go on the road. It wasn't easy. They did it because they wanted to be part of God's plan for Jesus. They are a model for all families who have to struggle with inconvenience, pain, loneliness and upset.

Children can identify with life's transitions and changes. It's part of their experience.

Focusing Experiences

Have you ever moved house yourself? Ever left your own home to move to a new neighbourhood? You know what's involved. You part company with your friends. You part company with familiar places, playgrounds, landmarks, shops, stores. It makes you feel sad and lonely. It's a lonely time.

For families who are moving out because of persecution there is the added fear of being arrested or killed.

For those who are on the move because of famine there is the fear of starvation, of dying, of hunger.

Or have you moved into a new school? A new classroom with a different set of classmates? That presents its own kind of difficulties. There is the fear of being rejected, the fear of not fitting in, the anxiety that is part of this new challenge.

Exploring the Word of God
Joseph and Mary took to the road with Jesus to escape persecution. They gathered a few belongings and set out for the border with Egypt. They were poor and had no powerful friends to protect them. It was a time of trouble for Mary and Joseph, of anxiety, of worry, of sleeplessness, of fear for their child Jesus. People had been killed on the road. People had been robbed. People had been arrested. They knew what they were facing. They took great caution and put up with the hardship because they wanted to do what they had to do for God. They wanted to be part of God's plan for the wonderful new things that were going to happen in the world.

Call of Faith
We are called to remember the Holy Family when our own family faces trouble, or has to move to a new place. Remembering their kind of courage, we can face the loss, the loneliness, the change, the newness, the upset. They felt that God was with them no matter what happened.

Call to action
Let's show cause with families who have to face upset.
Can you think of a way to make new pupils in the school welcome?
Let's make a prayer committing families who are suffering upset to the care of Jesus, Mary and Joseph.
Draw a picture of the Holy Family on the road facing their own kind of hardship.
Let's compose a ballad that tells the story of Jesus, Mary and Joseph finding a place of peace in a new land.

Solemnity of Mary

Gospel

A reading from the holy Gospel according to Luke (2:16-21)

So they hurried off and found Mary and Joseph and saw the baby lying in the manger. When the shepherds saw him, they told them what the angel had said about the child. All who heard it were amazed at what the shepherds said. Mary remembered all these things and thought deeply about them. The shepherds went back, singing praises to God for all they had heard and seen; it had been just as the angel had told them.

A week later, when the time came for the baby to be circumcised, he was named Jesus, the name which the angel had given him before he had been conceived.

This is the Gospel of the Lord

Overview

At Christmas time we honour Mary for giving us Jesus, our Saviour God. We formalise that desire to honour Mary by celebrating the Solemnity of Mary, the Mother of God.

There are two strands to the readings. The first is a presentation of Mary in a family context, as mother, Jewish mother. The second strand is more reflective of who Jesus is. The shepherds bear witness to the fact that this baby is marked out for greatness by God. The hand of God is on him. The angels of God are around him. He is the Saviour, Christ the Lord. And Mary is his mother. Mother of God.

Children show reverence, affection, honour by actions. They'll know that actions like having a march, turning out in crowds, making speeches, following the cortege, are ways of honouring special people among us. We can alert the children to the reason why Mary should be honoured. We can alert them to the long tradition in the Church of honouring Mary in the way of crowds, processions and speeches. This can be followed by our own procession, on this day, to honour Mary.

Focusing Experiences

Turn-out of crowds at an airport to honour or welcome a celebrity. Gathering of crowds in the centre of the city to hear speeches of tribute to the celebrity. Freedom of the city sometimes conferred on the celebrity.

A long tradition, going back over hundreds of years, of crowds gathering to honour Mary and ask for her help. Happens all over the world. People gather in small groups at street corner shrines or in their hundreds of thousands at world famous Marian Shrines to honour Mary and ask for her intercession.

Exploring the Word of God

These shepherds, made famous in today's gospel, were out in wind and rain. Out on the mountains. Knew lonely times. Stayed awake on dark nights, watching, guarding.

They had pleasant times too. They saw the sun rising behind the mountain and filling the valleys with the dawn light. They saw the flowers in the fields making their first uncertain appearance above the ground in the Spring and growing stronger with the gentle heat of the sun and coming into full bloom in the Summer.

They saw God's busy world at work and they admired God's handiwork. They blessed God for his world and everything in it.

They listened for God's voice. They listened for God's voice in the wind that whispered at night, in the trees that spoke with creaky voices, in the grass that swayed and moved to the secret messages written by God. They listened for the voice of God in the noisy streams that sped down the mountains like messengers possessed. And they listened and thanked God for everything God said.

They were men of God. They were blessed by God and could hear what God was saying.

And God spoke news to them of a baby born in a stable, the Christ child, the Saviour of the world, long promised by God to his people. And they understood, and praised God for remembering God's people. They left where they were and what they were doing and went, praising God, to the place where they could honour their Saviour. They found the Saviour, with his mother Mary, and they knelt before him and worshipped him.

They rose to their feet, blessed the woman, the mother of the Saviour, and made their way back to the mountain, thanking God for goodness and kindness beyond all expectation.

Call to Faith

We are called to show reverence, affection and honour for Mary, the Mother of God.

Call to Action

Organise a procession, a march, a gathering in Mary's honour (school grounds, church grounds, church building). Have speeches and prayers in Mary's honour. Sing her praises!

Make a dance that expresses, in movement and gesture, your tribute to Mary, Mother of God.

Make a small, medal-like decoration for your own room at home.

Second Sunday after Christmas

Gospel

A reading from the holy Gospel according to John (1:19-28)

The Jewish authorities in Jerusalem sent some priests and Levites to John, to ask him, 'Who are you?' John did not refuse to answer, but spoke out openly and clearly, saying, 'I am not the Messiah.' 'Who are you, then?' they asked, ' Are you Elijah?' 'No, I am not,' John answered. 'Are you the Prophet?' they asked. 'No,' he replied. 'Then tell us who you are,' they said. ' We have to take an answer back to those who sent us. What do you say about yourself?' John answered by quoting the prophet Isaiah: 'I am "the voice of someone shouting in the desert: Make straight a path for the Lord to travel!"' The messengers, who had been sent by the Pharisees, then asked John, 'If you are not the Messiah nor Elijah nor the Prophet, why do you baptize?' John answered, 'I baptize with water, but among you stands the one you do not know. He is coming after me, but I am not good enough even to untie his sandals.'

This is the Gospel of the Lord.

Overview

The focus is on Jesus. Jesus the Messiah is totally different. Different from even the best there is among God's friends. Different from John the Baptist and he was among the best. Today's gospel story is an effort to get a measure on the person of Jesus and who he really is for us.

Children have a sense of great people, of great leaders. When we say that Jesus was in a league on his own, they know what we are talking about.

Focusing Experiences

Stories of ordinary people who have been mistaken for kings or queens or great heroes. Stories of ordinary people in the street who have been mistaken for superstars or famous actresses. Can you imagine an ordinary girl walking into a supermarket and being mistaken for a famous actress or popular star? Can you imagine the excitement? People are delighted to have the famous actress among them. All too soon it is discovered that the ordinary girl cannot sing like the star or cannot act or dance like the star. The bubble bursts. All the excitement comes to nothing.

Exploring the Word of God

People were talking a lot about the Messiah. There was a sense of excitement in the air. People sensed that something wonderful was about to happen. People suspected that the Messiah was already among them.

But who was he? Some wise people put forward the name of John the Baptist. He was holy and good and a prophet as well. They said that John the Baptist was the Messiah promised by God. But John put an end to this rumour and said he was not the Messiah. He said they were mistaken. 'You've got it wrong,' he told them. 'You're way out.' He told them the Messiah was above and beyond anything he could ever be. He told them the Messiah would bring them into touch with the living God. 'With the Messiah among you, you will be truly walking with God himself.'

What John said caused even more stir and more excitement and more wondering. And the search was on, even more intensely, for God's Messiah. The people wanted to honour the Messiah more than anyone had ever been honoured before. But who could he be?

Call to Faith

We are called to honour Jesus as the Messiah. We are called to honour Jesus who has brought God among us. We are called to honour Jesus who has put us in touch with the Living God. We are called to honour Jesus who is our Lord.

Call to Action

Let's think of phrases or slogans that pay tribute to Jesus the Lord, God's Messiah among us.

Let's rework that statement of John the Baptist: 'I am not worthy to untie his sandals.' Put that in other words. Use other images to convey that meaning.

Sing a hymn of praise to Jesus the Lord.

Draw a picture of John the Baptist with the crowd milling around him thinking he might be the Messiah.

The Epiphany of the Lord

Gospel

A reading from the holy Gospel according to Matthew (2:1-12)

Jesus was born in the town of Bethlehem in Judaea, during the time when Herod was king. Soon afterwards, some men who studied the stars came from the east to Jerusalem and asked, 'Where is the baby born to be the King of the Jews? We saw his star when it came up in the east, and we have come to worship him.'

When Herod heard about this, he was very upset, and so was everyone else in Jerusalem. He called together all the chief priests and teachers of the Law and asked them, 'Where will the Messiah be born?' 'In the town of Bethlehem in Judaea,' they answered. 'For that is what the prophet wrote: "Bethlehem in the land of Judaea, you are by no means the least of the leading cities of Judah; for from you will come a leader who will guide my people Israel."'

So Herod called the visitors from the east to a secret meeting and found out from them the exact time the star had appeared. Then he sent them to Bethlehem with these instructions: 'Go and make a careful search for the child, and when you find him, let me know, so that I too may go and worship him.'

And so they left, and on their way they saw the same star they had seen in the east. When they saw it, how happy they were, what joy was theirs! It went ahead of them until it stopped over the place where the child was. They went into the house, and when they saw the child and his mother Mary, they knelt down and worshipped him. They brought out their gifts of gold, frankincense, and myrrh, and presented them to him.

Then they returned to their country by another road, since God had warned them in a dream not to go back to Herod.

This is the Gospel of the Lord.

Overview

Mary and Joseph were Jews. So were the shepherds. They knew the story of God's Messiah, the Saviour who was to come among God's people. The wise men from the East were strangers. Different from Mary and Joseph and the Shepherds. They had their own ideas. They were searching for their Saviour God.

Children identify with the adventure of the wise men. The story has all the ingredients of a fascinating tale: mystery, adventure, the East with its strange ways, journey by camel, and being guided by a mysterious star. It is also a story which gives a hint of God's plan to share his love with strangers. It's another level of mystery in this story for the children.

Focusing Experiences
Strangers who come a long way to pay honour to a great poet, playright or star. There was a visitor who came thousands of miles to visit the poet Yvteschenko in Moscow. 'I have come on a great journey to honour the man who writes such beautiful poety,' said the visitor. 'Your poetry has made such a difference to my life.' Visitors from far away lands who come to pay their respects to holy men or wise men. Strangers who come a long way to visit the Pope.

Exploring the Word of God.
Leaders from the East came to pay their respects to Jesus, their Saviour. The appeal of a Saviour reaches across mountains, valleys and frontiers to touch people in new and distant lands. Now strangers from the East were on the move to visit the Saviour. They came on a journey lasting many days to offer Jesus homage and honour. He is their Saviour too. They kneel before him and bow low. A tribute from strangers to the Saviour God. They came on a great journey to pay their respects to him who brought them face to face with the living God.

It wasn't an easy journey. It was long and tedious and Herod tried to entrap them to betray Jesus. But they fulfilled their task and completed their quest. They went home by another route to avoid the interest of Herod. They were the first strangers to experience God's love through Jesus. Their adventure lives on forever.

Call of Faith
We are called from north, south, east and west to honour Jesus. From the mountains we are called. From the villages. From the towns. From the cities. From the countryside. From the desert. From the rainforests. From the plains. From the islands. We are all called to worship Jesus our Lord.

Call to Action
Honour Jesus in the crib in as many languages as you have people in the parish to speak them. Translate a statement like: All the nations gather from the ends of the earth to worship the Lord.
Honour Jesus with a hymn in a foreign language.
With appropriate ritual, raise flags of many nations around the crib.
Sing a hymn like *All the Nations*.

The Baptism of the Lord

(First Sunday in Ordinary Time)

Gospel

A reading from the holy Gospel according to Matthew (3:13-17)

At that time Jesus arrived from Galilee and came to John at the Jordan to be baptized by him. But John tried to make him change his mind. 'I ought to be baptized by you,' John said, 'and yet you have come to me!'

But Jesus answered him, 'Let it be so for now. For in this way we shall do all that God requires.' So John agreed.

As soon as Jesus was baptized, he came up out of the water. Then heaven was opened to him, and he saw the Spirit of God coming down like a dove and alighting on him. Then a voice said from heaven, 'This is my own dear Son, with whom I am pleased.'

This is the Gospel of the Lord

Overview

Firstly, Matthew's gospel story of the baptism of Jesus in the Jordan makes a strong point about the humanity of Jesus. Jesus walks into the waters of the Jordan like the rest of God's people asking to be washed and made whole before a loving, merciful and forgiving God. It is declaration that Jesus is one of us.

Secondly, the story of the baptism presents the credentials of Jesus. He is publicly declared to be the Son of God. Matthew sees this as a fitting beginning to Jesus' public ministry among God's people. Jesus is indeed the awaited Messiah.

Thirdly, this gospel story creates a sympathetic context for the practice of Christian baptism.

With children it is best to focus on the credentials of Jesus. This kind of exploration helps them to get to know Jesus. Helps them to see where Jesus fits into God's plan for his people. Helps them to become more aware of Jesus' relationship with God the Father.

Focusing Experiences

A car driver is given a licence before going on the road as a fully qualified driver. The driver is declared fit and suitable for the job by people who know about driving. A footballer is picked for the First Team by selectors who know about football. A pilot is granted a licence before flying an aeroplane. The pilot is declared suitable by people who know about flying. A scientist has to be declared fit and suitable to undertake difficult and dangerous experiments. The scientist is given clearance by people who know about these things.

Exploring the Word of God

The Father gave Jesus the 'go ahead' to teach and preach to the people about God. It happened at the baptism of Jesus in the Jordan. It was a good time to get the 'go ahead' from the Father. Lots of people around – very public place; crowds there to hear everything, and to notice everything.

Jesus was on the bank of the river Jordan attending a service of prayer, penance and baptism. Like others he was in a queue of people who were opening their hearts to God and walking into the waters of the river to present themselves before John the Baptist.

John the Baptist was baptising the people in the water. It was a way of giving God's blessing and friendship to people who asked for it. When their turn came, people were taken by John and his assistants and lowered into the water. For a split second they were covered in the water. They were delighted to be covered by the flowing water because they hoped and prayed that all their badness would be left behind in the water and swept away by God. Each person who was baptised by John came out of the water smiling and feeling good before God and promising to do their very best to live in friendship with God.

When his turn came, Jesus stood before John and asked for God's blessing and baptism. He waited to be lowered into the water. When John the Baptist saw Jesus he took fright because he knew in his heart of hearts that he was talking to the Son of God. John the Baptist begged to be excused. He said he wasn't worthy. He said it wasn't right for him to baptise Jesus. But Jesus insisted. "I want to be baptised. Lower me into the water, John. Baptise me with God's baptism. Bless me with God's blessing. Baptise me for what I have to do."

Reluctanlty John lowered Jesus into the water. As he was helped back onto his feet a voice spoke from heaven: "This is my Son, the beloved. Listen to him". It was the Father marking Jesus out for the mission. It was the Father giving him the 'go ahead' for his work in the towns and villages he was going to visit in the days and weeks ahead. It was the Father saying that Jesus was fit and suitable for the mission. It was the Father saying that Jesus was the person for the job.

Call to Faith

We are called to recognise Jesus as the Son of God. We are called to welcome him as he comes on his mission among us.

Call to action

Arrange a Baptismal renewal service. Compose a service for children and families – a family renewal.

Have a ceremonial blessing with water to remind those present of their baptism and the road of commitment that it set them on.

First Sunday of Lent

Gospel

A reading from the holy Gospel according to Matthew (4: 1-11)
Then the Spirit led Jesus into the desert to be tempted by the devil. After spending forty days and nights without food, Jesus was hungry. Then the devil came to him and said, 'If you are God's Son, order these stones to turn into bread.' But Jesus answered, 'The scripture says, "Man cannot live on bread alone, but needs every word that God speaks."' Then the devil took Jesus to Jerusalem, the Holy City, and sat him on the highest point of the Temple, and said to him, 'If you are God's Son, throw yourself down, for the scripture says, "God will give orders to his angels about you; they will hold you up with their hands so that not even your feet will be hurt on these stones."' Jesus answered, 'But the scripture also says, "Do not put the Lord your God to the test."' Then the devil took Jesus to a very high mountain and showed him all the kingdoms of the world in their greatness. 'All this I will give you,' the devil said, 'if you kneel down and worship me.' Then Jesus answered, 'Go away, Satan! The scripture says, "Worship the Lord your God and serve only God."' Then the devil left Jesus; and angels came and helped him.
This is the Gospel of the Lord

Overview

Jesus is tempted. He struggles. He fights temptation. Jesus knows that the evil way can be very attractive. The good way can be difficult. Jesus shows us how to face down evil and take the good way to heart.

Children experience temptation. They struggle too. The story of Jesus' temptation strikes a chord with them.

Focusing Experiences

Being tempted to tell lies.
Being tempted to make fun of someone.
Being tempted to be bossy and overbearing.
Being tempted to steal.
Being tempted to make trouble.
Being tempted to cheat at games.
Being tempted to fight in a mean way with friends.
Being tempted to be selfish.
Remember a time you were tempted. To cheat. To lie. To hurt someone. To be disagreeable. To make trouble. Remember the struggle. Remember how it felt. It seemed easy to give in. It seemed easy to say 'yes' to the temptation. That's the thing about temptations: they dress themselves

up to look better than they are. It doesn't seem so wrong to give in to temptation, to do what is suggested. It almost seems to be right. That's the way temptation works. Temptations jolly you along to do something that's wrong.

Temptations convince you someone deserved a cutting lash from your tongue. Persuade you it is alright to make trouble. Give you the feeling your friend deserves every bit of it. Temptations dress up in pretty colours to hide the evil beneath. Behind words and feelings that seem reasonable, temptations suggest actions that must be resisted.

Exploring the Word of God
Jesus was tempted. The temptations were dressed up in words and dreams that seemed very attractive. He was tempted three times. Each time a dream that had an appeal. He resisted with some difficulty. He resisted. He faced down the temptation. He said, 'No.'

Call of Faith
We are called to resist temptation. We are called to recognise that temptations can attract, allure, persuade, appeal, convince. But we have to resist. We are called to resist. We are called to join in the fight against evil. We are called to spread goodness and resist evil. We are called to stand shoulder to shoulder with Jesus against evil. We are called to support him in his great quest to spread love. We are called to work with him to give love a chance.

Call to Action
Find phrases that temptations are often packaged in:
  Ah, go on, it's ok!
  It's nothing really. Do it!
  They deserve it!
  It's only a bit of fun!
  It's all right. Do it!
  No one will hear about it. Do it!
  Nobody will get hurt. It's your own business!
  Don't listen. You've heard that before! Go on!

Imagine some stories of people your own age resisting temptation.
Talk to Jesus as he is being tempted and tell him why he mustn't give in.
Do a dance symbolising the temptations of Jesus.
Sing a hymn of praise to Jesus who leads us along the right path.

Second Sunday of Lent

Gospel

A reading from the holy Gospel according to Matthew (17:1-9)

Jesus took with him Peter and the brothers James and John and led them up a high mountain where they were alone. As they looked on, a change came over Jesus: his face was shining like the sun, and his clothes were dazzling white. Then the three disciples saw Moses and Elijah talking with Jesus. So Peter spoke up and said to Jesus, 'Lord, how good it is that we are here! If you wish, I will make three tents here, one for you, one for Moses, and one for Elijah.'

While he was talking, a shining cloud came over them, and a voice from the cloud said, 'This is my own dear Son, with whom I am pleased – listen to him!'

When the disciples heard the voice, they were so terrified that they threw themselves face downwards on the ground. Jesus came to them and touched them. 'Get up,' he said, 'Don't be afraid!' So they looked up and saw no one there but Jesus.

This is the Gospel of the Lord.

Overview

The apostles are overcome by their experience of seeing Jesus, literally in a new light. They see him, for an instant, in his full glory. They see the God-ness in him. It takes their breath away.

Children should not have a problem dealing with this manifestation of the divine in Jesus. They have a sense of mystery while we adults tend to be cynical or too 'scientific' in our approach to life.

Focusing Experiences

Did you ever hear a story of a quiet girl or woman who reveals herself for an instant as a hero (in a car crash, a swimming accident, a fire)?

Or a child who for a short time shows greatness and courage beyond their years?

Or a child who, in a short act, reveals a wonderful and hidden talent for singing or acting or dancing?

Or a child who races up a sportstrack in a time that shows extraordinary talent?

Or a child who makes a speech that is a 'knock-out'?

Or a child who shows a special genius in answering exam questions?

Exploring the Word of God

The disciples walked the roads of Galilee with Jesus. They were friends.

They shared together. They talked together. They laughed together. They knew Jesus. They thought they knew everything about him as friends always seem to about each other. But nothing could have prepared them for the shock they got when they saw a new side to Jesus. In a quiet place on a mountain slope they were treated to a vision of Jesus as God's Son. They were dazzled and shocked and overcome. It gave them pause for thought. They could hardly take it in. It was an experience they were not likely to forget. It stayed with them forever.

Call to Faith
Jesus may seem ordinary. He is our friend. He is our leader. He is one of us. But the fact that he is Lord can never be hidden. We bow before him. We are called to say in prayer, 'Jesus I adore you.' We are called to honour Jesus our friend as Jesus our Lord.

Call to Action
Pray to Jesus as Lord.
Sing to Jesus as Lord.
Draw Jesus transfigured and revealed for an instant in all his divine glory.

Third Sunday of Lent

Gospel

A reading from the holy Gospel according to John 4:5-42

In Samaria Jesus came to a town named Sychar. Jacob's well was there, and Jesus, tired out by the journey, sat down by the well. A Samaritan woman came to draw some water, and Jesus said to her, 'Give me a drink of water.' The woman answered, 'You are a Jew, and I am a Samaritan, so how can you ask me for a drink?' Jesus answered, 'If you only knew what God gives and who it is that is asking you for a drink, you would ask him, and he would give you life-giving water. Whoever drinks this water will be thirsty again, but whoever drinks the water that I will give him will never be thirsty again. The water that I will give him will become in him a spring which will provide him with life-giving water and give him eternal life.' 'Sir,' the woman said, 'Give me that water! Then I will never be thirsty again, nor will I have to come here to draw water.' 'Go and call your husband,' Jesus said to her, 'and come back.' 'I haven't got a husband,' she answered. Jesus replied, 'You are right when you say you haven't got a husband. You have been married to five men, and the man you live with now is not really your husband. You have told me the truth.' 'I see you are a prophet, Sir,' the woman said. 'I know that the Messiah will come, and when he comes, he will tell us everything.' Jesus answered, 'I am he, who am talking with you.' So they left the town and went to Jesus. Many of the Samaritans in that town believed in Jesus because the woman had said, 'He told me everything I have ever done.' They begged him to stay with them, and Jesus stayed there two days. Many more believed because of his message, and they said, 'We believe now, not because of what you have said, but because we ourselves have heard him, and we know that he really is the Saviour of the world.' This is the Gospel of the Lord.

Overview

From water that people drink to give life and health, the talk between Jesus and the woman gets more and more spiritual. They talk of the life and health of the spirit in us. She hears and understands what Jesus is saying because she is looking for God and God's ways.

While children are most at home in talk that concerns concrete and practical situations, they also have a sense of deeper things, of things of the spirit.

Focusing Experiences

Were you ever out in the open at night? Did you ever talk about the stars and go on to talk about deeper things like God and God's world?

Did you ever have a quiet talk about sport and go on to talk about deeper things like courage, commitment, dedication which are qualities shown by some players or sports people?

Did you ever talk about death and begin to worry and feel sad about the future death of friends?

Did you ever talk about love?

Exploring the Word of God

Jesus and the woman began a conversation about water and thirst which would be natural enough on a hot day after a walk in the heat. It was natural because the two of them were standing at the well and could hear the splash of buckets drawing out the water.

But the conversation went on to deeper things like the thirst people feel for God. The thirst for God is not in the throat, but in the heart and the mind. The woman had that thirst for God. She had a longing for God. She wanted to have God in her life. She wanted to be close to God.

She was completely taken up by what Jesus was saying. She felt she was in touch with a great teacher. And she got the best out of him because she asked him questions with a twinkle in her eye and a laugh on her lips. Very good humoured she was, and interested in every single word he was saying. As she talked to him she was trying to figure out who this man might be. He seemed to know so much about God. A great teacher? Certainly! More maybe? A prophet? Yes! And good heavens, maybe the Messiah himself! No one could speak with such sureness about God unless that person was the Messiah! She excused herself pleasantly and walked quickly back to the town. Her news for everyone was, 'You know, I think I've just met the Messiah. Come and meet him, and judge for yourselves.'

Call of Faith

We are called to hear the deeper things Jesus is saying about God. We are called to hear that in our hearts and minds we have a thirst for God. We are called to hear that Jesus will show us a way to satisfy that thirst for God.

Call to Action

When holy men or women in their monasteries chant their prayers we sometimes feel a longing for God.

Listen (on tape) to some of their beautiful monastic chants. Follow this with spoken prayers of longing for God.

Honour Jesus who leads us to find the God of our hearts.

Sing a hymn of praise to Jesus.

Have a few moments' experience of meditation with God.

Fourth Sunday of Lent

Gospel

A reading from the holy Gospel according to John (9:1,6-9.13-17.34-38)

As Jesus was walking along, he saw a man who had been born blind. Jesus spat on the ground and made some mud with the spittle; he rubbed the mud on the man's eyes and said, 'Go and wash your face in the Pool of Siloam.' (This name means 'Sent.') So the man went, washed his face, and came back seeing.

His neighbours then, and the people who had seen him begging before this, asked, 'Isn't this the man who used to sit and beg? 'Some said, 'He is the one,' but others said, 'No he isn't; he just looks like him.' So the man himself said, 'I am the man.'

Then they took to the Pharisees the man who had been blind. The day that Jesus made the mud and cured him of his blindness was a Sabbath. The Pharisees then asked the man again how he had received his sight. He told them, 'He put some mud on my eyes; I washed my face, and now I can see.' Some of the Pharisees said, 'The man who did this cannot be from God, for he does not obey the Sabbath law.' Others, however, said, 'How could a man who is a sinner perform such miracles as these?' And there was a division among them.

So the Pharisees asked the man once more, 'You say he cured you of your blindness – well, what do you say about him?' 'He is a prophet,' the man answered. They answered, 'You were born and brought up in sin – and you are trying to teach us?' And they expelled him from the synagogue.

When Jesus heard what had happened, he found the man and asked him, 'Do you believe in the Son of Man?' The man answered, 'Tell me who he is, Sir, so that I can believe in him!' Jesus said to him, 'You have already seen him and he is the one who is talking with you now.' 'I believe, Lord!' the man said, and knelt down before Jesus.

This is the Gospel of the Lord.

Overview

Jesus does a sign. He cures a blind man. It should have opened everyone's eyes to who Jesus was. Some people in high positions were enraged that he did a sign. It didn't please them that people were immediately connecting the sign with God and asking if Jesus was God's Messiah. Jesus didn't fit in with their ideas of the Messiah. He didn't fit in with the picture in their mind of the Messiah. He was too ordinary. So they denied the sign, couldn't admit it ever happened. The blind man who was cured didn't have any trouble recognising what the sign meant. He threw himself at Jesus' feet and honoured him as the Messiah.

Children relate to the world of the immediate, the obvious, the direct. However, they powerfully intuit the world of signs. This intuition can be externalised with a little talk and a little exploration. And they rather enjoy puzzling out the meaning of signs.

Focusing Experiences
Making sense of signs:
Signs of beauty,
Signs of love,
Signs of upset,
Signs of fatigue,
Signs of happiness.

Are you good at making sense of signs? Do you know when your mother or father or teacher is angry? Can you see the signs? Do you know when a friend is upset? Can you see and understand the signs? Do you sense when someone is very happy?
Have you seen signs of beauty? What effect had it on you?
Do you know the signs of love? How do signs of love help people to communicate. What do the signs of love say?
It is clear we live in a world of signs. The signs are obvious enough and straightforward enough. We see the signs. We can't miss them. But signs tell a deeper story. We look at signs with our eyes or hear them with our ears. Then we read the deeper meaning of the signs with our hearts and our feelings. We have to read the signs with our minds. Figure out the deeper meaning.

Exploring the Word of God
Jesus gave the people a sign about the Messiah. He cured a blind man. People immediately went looking for the deeper meaning. They said, 'This is a sign! What we have seen is the work of God's Messiah. It means that Jesus is the Messiah. It must mean that.'

Some of the leaders didn't want to give a second thought to the idea that Jesus might be the Messiah. They figured he would be a complete let-down as the Messiah. He couldn't be the Messiah. Nazareth, that village! No Messiah could come from Nazareth! And for that matter he was only a second rate carpenter! Too busy talking and preaching! Even his talk was very ordinary! He talked about everyday things! Sheep and shepherds and fig trees. Far too ordinary for a Messiah! A preacher, with dust on his feet! He didn't have a style that would impress anyone. No popular appeal. The Messiah had to be better than that. So they denied the sign. 'There was no sign,' they said. 'It's all a lie, a bluff. Make-believe! There's nothing to it. No sign at all. End of story. Everyone go home!'

But people wouldn't go home. Especially the man who had been cured. He shouted out what a great and marvellous thing had happened to him. He told again and again how he had been cured by Jesus. The people believed God had given a sign. They wondered and wondered who Jesus was? The man who had once been blind didn't hesitate. He was convinced Jesus was the Messiah. That's how he read the sign. And nothing, just nothing was going to change his mind.

Call of Faith
We are called to follow Jesus like the man who once was blind. We are called to see Jesus as the sign of God among us.

Call to Action
Arrange for the man who once was blind to give a press conference. Have questions prepared.
Sing or recite a ballad that tells the story of the blind man.
Find phrases that capture the feelings of the blind man as he tries to convince the people that Jesus is God's Messiah.

Fifth Sunday of Lent

Gospel
A reading from the holy Gospel according to John (11:3-7.17:20-27,33-45)
Mary arrived where Jesus was and, as soon as she saw him, she fell at his feet. 'Lord,' she said, 'if you had been here, my brother would not have died!'

Jesus saw her weeping, and he saw how the people who were with her were weeping also; his heart was touched, and he was deeply moved. 'Where have you buried him?' he asked them. 'Come and see, Lord,' they answered. Jesus wept.

Deeply moved once more, Jesus went to the tomb, which was a cave with a stone placed at the entrance. 'Take the stone away!' Jesus ordered. They took the stone away. Jesus looked up and said, 'I thank you, Father, that you listen to me. I know that you always listen to me, but I say this for the sake of the people here, so that they will believe that you sent me.'

After he had said this, he called out in a loud voice, 'Lazarus, come out!' He came out, his hands and feet wrapped in grave clothes, and with a cloth round his face. 'Untie him,' Jesus told them, 'and let him go.'
This is the Gospel of the Lord

Overview

Who is Jesus? Another sign is given in today's reading. Who could this man be who raises people from the dead? Friend? Messiah from God? Who? For children it is an opportunity to continue to explore and puzzle out the signs. It is an opportunity to familiarise themselves with deeper aspects of Jesus' personality.

Focusing Experiences

Signs have meanings. A beautiful scene can tell us about the treasures of colour that lie before us, inviting our admiration. A beautiful scene can be a feast for the eyes. It can be many things. Is it a sign of God's handiwork? Is it evidence that our world is God's world, God's handiwork? When we look at something beautiful are we getting a glimpse, a fleeting glimpse, a reminder, a sign of God's beauty?

Exploring the Word of God

Jesus did signs like healing the man who was blind. But more follows. Another story today. Another sign is given. Jesus raises Lazarus from the dead. Shock and disbelief 138eft people with their mouths open. Who could he be who raised people from the dead? What was going on? What did it signify? What did it point to? But shock or no shock, people had to consider the possibility that Jesus was indeed the Messiah from God. That question stared them in the face as Lazarus walked alive from the tomb of the dead. If Jesus was the Messiah then God was among them. If God was among them then everything the people thought worth wanting in life and worth waiting for was within their grasp. Their religion said, and they learned this on their mother's knee, that to be alive for the day of the Messiah was an honour beyond all honours and a privilege beyond all privileges. Was Jesus the Messiah? Some were sure. Some hesitated. Some turned away.

Call to Faith

We are called to see the sign of the raising of Lazarus as a sign by which we can recognise God's Messiah. The hand of God was in it. It points to the presence of God. The power of God was in Jesus when he did it. It is a sign of who Jesus is. He is God's Messiah. The sign tells us about Jesus. The sign tells us that Jesus brings God among us.

Call to Action

Compose a ballad of Jesus and Lazarus.

Write up interview questions that will be directed at Mary and Martha.

Do a news report from the scene. Try to reflect the opinions of Mary, Martha, the bystanders, and also those who opposed Jesus.

Passion Sunday

The passion of Our Lord Jesus Christ according to Matthew (26:14-27:66)

Please refer to your lectionary for this reading which is very long.

Overview
Jesus didn't give up on God or on us. He remained calm when the agony should have driven him to raving madness. He remained at peace when the pain and the passion of suffering should have caused him to curse his captors in bitter anger. He never lost hope when everything seemed hopeless. The suffering didn't seem able to destroy him. He held on and held out for God's sake and for our sake.

The Passion of Jesus often touches children at a first level, a level of pain, of suffering, of courage, of sympathy. We can enrich children's understsanding if we can bring them to the second level of seeing the Passion of Jesus as an act of love, of self-giving. Jesus' passion and death was an act of love of gigantic proportions.

Focusing Experiences
A time you were impressed by courage in the face of terrible disaster.
A time you were impressed by peace and gentleness in desperate circumstances.
A time you were impressed by a refusal to give in when nothing was left.
Have you read lines from Shackleton's diary as he journeyed towards the South Pole? Were you impressed with his calm and dignified courage?
Are you impressed with the courage of hostages when you hear of their ordeals?
Are you impressed with newsmen who venture into danger to bring out news?
Have you seen pictures on TV of mothers in war zones suffering desperate hardship for the sake of their children?
Have you heard stories of people who put themselves in danger for their friends?
Have you heard of rescue attempts that involved exceptional risk and exceptional danger?
Have you heard of people who died attempting to save friend or family?

Exploring the Word of God
People who saw how Jesus suffered were impressed. They saw calmness and gentleness. They saw a man of peace. And he had no reason to be gentle or at peace. The suffering was unbearable. Yet he bore it because

he seemed almost to be concentrating on other things. Concentrating on God whom he loved with a great love. Concentrating on us. He was making his life over to God as a gift of love for us. The army captain who watched it all as he escorted Jesus on the journey from the courthouse to the hill of execution on Calvary was very impressed. He couldn't get over the love that seemed to flow from this man, this supposed criminal, condemned to die on a cross. When his duty at the cross ended that day he said with conviction, 'This man was indeed the son of God.'

The good thief was so impressed that he put his faith and his future in Jesus' hands. And the followers who watched from a distance sensed that Jesus was suffering what he was suffering for them.

Call to Faith
We are called to honour, praise and thank Jesus for the extraordinarily generous love he showed for us on the cross.

Call to Action
Play meditative music, soulful music, serious music, to accompany Jesus on his way to Calvary.

Walk the Stations of the Cross with Jesus. Write a script for the Stations with the recurring theme of thanking Jesus for his love.

Carry the cross in procession. Worship the cross on which Jesus the Saviour died for us.

Thank Jesus in prayer for the love he showed for us on the cross.

Easter Sunday

Gospel
A reading from the holy Gospel according to John (20:1-9)
Early on Sunday morning, while it was still dark, Mary Magdalene went to the tomb and saw that the stone had been taken away from the entrance. She went running to Simon Peter and the other disciple, whom Jesus loved, and told them, 'They have taken the Lord from the tomb, and we don't know where they have put him!' Then Peter and the other disciple went to the tomb. The two of them were running, but the other disciple ran faster than Peter and reached the tomb first. He bent over and saw the linen wrappings, but he did not go in. Behind him came Simon Peter, and he went straight into the tomb. He saw the linen wrappings lying there and the cloth which had been round Jesus' head. It was not lying with the linen wrappings but was rolled up by itself. Then the other disciple, who had reached the tomb first, also went in; he saw and believed. (They still did not understand the scripture which said that he must rise from death.)
This is the Gospel of the Lord

Overview
The dead body of Jesus is not in the tomb. Mary and the apostles are witnesses to that. The empty tomb took them completely by surprise. They were taken aback, surprised, shocked even. And they began to question and to hope. They began to feel that something wonderful had happened.

We wish to introduce the children to the Risen Jesus. It helps if we encourage them to feel and think and be amazed and excited as the first disciples were at the unfolding of events which began with the discovery of the empty tomb.

Focusing Experiences
Did you ever get a surprise which seemed to make no sense?
Did you ever meet with the unexpected?
Did you ever meet someone completely out of the blue in a most unexpected way?
Did anything ever happen to you which was just amazing, unbelievable?
Did anything ever happen to you which was totally different from what you were expecting?

Exploring the Word of God
Mary went to the tomb expecting to find the body of Jesus there. She was going to anoint the body and prepare it in a worthy manner for its final

sleep in death. Anointing was a funeral custom, a way of showing respect for the dead. A final farewell.

But the stone which covered the entrance was rolled back and the tomb was empty. Mary went running for help. For consolation. She wanted someone to tell her what was going on. As soon as she told the disciples, Peter and John, about the empty tomb, they came running back with her. They all stared and stared at the empty tomb. Slowly, they began to realise that a great miracle had taken place. Somehow Jesus was no longer dead. God had given him life.

Call to Faith
Jesus is alive. We greet Jesus our Risen Lord. We greet the Lord of life.

Call to Action
Easter hymns of praise to the Risen Jesus.
Exhuberant festive music.
Colour and lights.
Speeches, songs, greetings.
A thank-you to God in prayer for the Risen Jesus.

Second Sunday of Easter

Gospel

A reading from the holy Gospel according to John (20:19-31)

One of the twelve disciples, Thomas (called the Twin), was not with them when Jesus came. So the other disciples told him, 'We have seen the Lord!' Thomas said to them, 'Unless I see the scars of the nails in his hands and put my finger on those scars and my hand in his side, I will not believe!'

A week later the disciples were together again indoors, and Thomas was with them. The doors were locked, but Jesus came and stood among them and said, 'Peace be with you.' Then he said to Thomas, 'Put your finger here, and look at my hands; then stretch out your hand and put it in my side. Stop your doubting, and believe!' Thomas answered him, 'My Lord and my God!' Jesus said to him, 'Do you believe because you see me? How happy are those who believe without seeing me!'

This is the Gospel of the Lord

Overview

Faith has to do with the feelings of the heart as well as the evidence of eyes and ears. Thomas wanted the evidence of eyes and ears before he could believe in the Risen Jesus. Jesus reminded him not to depend just on the evidence of eyes and ears but to listen to the voice of God with his heart.

We introduce the children to Thomas who insisted on first-hand evidence of the presence of the Risen Jesus. We help them to look beyond the experience of eyes and ears to the experience of the heart.

Focusing Experiences

Why do you believe a trusted friend?
Why do you believe your parents?
Why do you believe your teachers?
Why do you believe your priest?

Exploring the Word of God

Thomas wanted to believe the good news that Jesus was risen. But it didn't make sense to him. Jesus, dead, then alive. The other friends told Thomas they had seen the Risen Jesus. Actually seen him. They said they spoke to Jesus. They said they saw Jesus with their own eyes. They said they would swear to him that it was Jesus. They pleaded with him to believe. They went over and over their stories telling him exactly what they had seen; when, where, how. Everything. And the truth of their stories

---

was in their eyes and in their words. But Thomas couldn't accept their word and their stories. He couldn't believe his friends. 'I must see the Risen Jesus,' he said. 'I must lay my hand on him. I must touch him. I must speak to him. Otherwise I cannot believe'.

Then Jesus stood with him. Face to face. Very close. Only a breath away. Jesus spoke to Thomas who was wide-eyed with wonder. Thomas bowed his head and said simply, 'My Lord and my God'.

Jesus said, 'Blessed are those who believe without seeing.' It was a rebuke to Thomas. It was a caution, a plea to Thomas to give his heart a chance, as well as his eyes and ears.

Call to Faith
We are called to have faith in Jesus. We are called to open our hearts to the story of Jesus we hear from parents, teachers and priests.

Call to Action
Songs of belief in the Risen Jesus.

Expressions of confidence in the Risen Jesus.

Words (speeches, letters) of thanks to our parents, priests and teachers for handing on to us their faith in the Risen Jesus.

A litany which begins: 'We believe...'

A poster expressing our faith in the Risen Jesus (words and art).

Third Sunday of Easter

Gospel

A reading from the holy Gospel according to Luke (24:13-35)

On that same day, two of Jesus' followers were going to a village named Emmaus, about eleven kilometres from Jerusalem, and they were talking to each other about all the things that had happened. As they talked and discussed, Jesus himself drew near and walked along with them; they saw him, but somehow did not recognise him. Jesus said to them, 'What are you talking about to each other, as you walk along?'

They stood still, with sad faces. One of them, named Cleopas, asked him, 'Are you the only visitor in Jerusalem who doesn't know the things that have been happening there these last few days?' 'What things?' he asked. 'The things that happened to Jesus of Nazareth,' they answered, 'This man was a prophet and was considered by God and by all the people to be powerful in everything he said and did. Our chief priests and rulers handed him over to be sentenced to death, and he was crucified. And we had hoped that he would be the one who was going to set Israel free! Besides all that, this is the third day since it happened. Some of the women of our group surprised us; they went at dawn to the tomb, but could not find his body. They came back saying they had seen a vision of angels who told them that he is alive. Some of our group went to the tomb and found it exactly as the women had said, but they did not see him.'

Then Jesus said to them, 'How foolish you are, how slow you are to believe everything the prophets said! Was it not necessary for the Messiah to suffer these things and then to enter his glory?' And Jesus explained to them what was said about himself in all the Scriptures, beginning with the books of Moses and the writings of all the prophets.

As they came near the village to which they were going, Jesus acted as if he were going farther; but they held him back, saying, 'Stay with us; the day is almost over and it is getting dark.' So he went in to stay with them. He sat down to eat with them, took the bread, and said the blessing; then he broke the bread and gave it to them. Then their eyes were opened and they recognised him, but he disappeared from their sight. They said to each other, 'Wasn't it like a fire burning in us when he talked to us on the road and explained the Scriptures to us?'

They got up at once and went back to Jerusalem, where they found the eleven disciples gathered together with the others and saying, 'The Lord is risen indeed! He has appeared to Simon!'

The two then explained to them what had happened on the road, and how they had recognised the Lord when he broke the bread.

This is the Gospel of the Lord

Overview

It's a story of sadness (they were downcast). Then of learning (they began to understand the meaning of the scriptures). Then of joy in the presence of the Risen Lord.

This gospel story has strong eucharisitic connections (assembly, the sharing of the word, and the sharing of the meal).

With children it might be best to explore these connections in a catechetical setting. In the homily we should simply try to give a feel of the presence of the Risen Lord to the two downcast disciples whose sad feelings turned first to consternation and then excitement and joy when they recognised the Risen Lord. The Risen Jesus is the kind of person who lifts our hearts, gives us something to sing about.

Focusing Experiences

Did you ever feel downhearted, then meet someone who helped you to understand things a bit better? Then with that person's help you get your bounce back and you're ready for anything again. Friends often help us through a bad patch of doubt or worry or hurt.

Parents often talk us through something that is getting us down – feeling left out, worrying about what we consider to be a personal defect, or physical defect, or fear of failure, or fear of embarrassment and any of the other concerns that bother us.

Counsellors often help a person through a pain or worry that is really blocking that person's growth and happiness. Have you ever talked to a counsellor or seen counsellors at work in television stories and dramas?

Exploring the Word of God

Two disciples were on the road out of Jerusalem on the way to the village of Emmaus. They were gloomy and sad. Their Master, Jesus, had been crucified. The hopes they had shared with him of changing the world, of making God better known, of spreading love, seemed to have been dashed. It was all over. The end for them and their hopes and dreams.

They talked as they walked. They hadn't much to say. But they did speak sadly of how things hadn't worked out for them. They wondered if it might have been different. How it could have been different.

They were joined by a stranger who was also walking the road. He was very pleasant and seemed to be immediately sensitive to the way they were feeling. He wasn't a bit intrusive, and was actually very good company. They explained the way they were feeling and apologised for having so little to say. But he seemed to understand their feelings. He talked very openly to them. He seemed very interested in hearing their story and encouraged them to talk about the great hopes they had and the wonderful dream they shared with Jesus of changing the world. He asked them many questions and listened very attentively as they answered. In his own way he put some new ideas to them. He did it in a gentle way and was in no way telling them their business. He reminded them of things they had almost forgotten. He pointed out things from the Bible that he thought they should consider. He lifted their spirits. It was clear to them that this was a man of understanding and learning. It was clear to them that this was a man who knew God's ways.

When they got to the village of Emmaus they invited him to have supper with them. They wanted to have the pleasure of entertaining this new and helpful friend to a little hospitality and a little food around a warm fire. And maybe more talk.

They sat down for the meal. He said the grace. He took the bread and blessed it and shared it out among them just as Jesus used to do. At that instant they recognised the man. It was the Risen Jesus. They were dumbfounded and delighted. And then he was gone from them.

When they got over the shock they paid their bill, cancelled the rooms they had booked for the night and left quickly. It was a dark night outside but the moon and stars were shining. They decided to walk back to Jerusalem even at this late hour. They planned to rouse the other disciples to share the good news that they had met the Risen Jesus.

Call to Faith
We are called to meet the Risen Jesus. He lifts our hearts. At Mass we gather together. We hear the words of Jesus. We behold him in the bread that is broken and shared out among us at Holy Communion. We sing. We celebrate.

Call to Action
Review the parts of the Mass which seem to be paralleled in today's gospel story: The Assembly, The Word of God, The breaking of Bread.
This might be done by way of special introductory words or commentary. Make posters, with captions to explain the importance of each of these parts of the Mass.
Sing a joyful song to the Risen Jesus.
Imagine and write a story of someone who tells Jesus about a worry that's bothering them.

Fourth Sunday of Easter

Gospel
A reading from the holy Gospel according to John (10:1-10)
Jesus said, 'I am telling you the truth: the man who does not enter the sheepfold by the gate, but climbs in some other way, is a thief and a robber. The man who goes in through the gate is the shepherd of the sheep. The gatekeeper opens the gate for him; the sheep hear his voice as he calls his own sheep by name, and he leads them out. When he has brought them out, he goes ahead of them, and the sheep follow him, because they know his voice. They will not follow someone else; instead they will run away from such a person, because they do not know his voice.'
This is the Gospel of the Lord

Overview
The Bible uses the imagery of the relationship between sheep and shepherd to tell us about the dependable, lasting and permanent relationship we can have with the Risen Jesus. Jesus is no 'Will o the Wisp', no con-man, no passing flavour of the month. He is solid, dependable and loves us.

With children it is worth making the effort to explore the sheep/shepherd relationship even though that imagery had its real home in the Bible lands.

Focusing Experiences
Explore what we know about con-artists (con-men, con-women)/ sweet-talkers / smoothies.

A con-artist talks sweetly. Some people are taken in by the talk. It sounds so convincing. You almost have to believe it. It all fits together. A con-artist could persuade you that black was white. That's what they're good at. Persuading. Making you see things their way. Wanting to help you. Convincing you. Conning you.

People have been known to give money to con-artists to buy land or buy a bargain. Even their life-savings. It sounds ridiculous, but it's true. The con-artist always disappears with the money and is never heard of again. Disappears into thin air. Staying around means being found out. Pick up what they can with their smooth talk and then skip out of town. That is the way it is with con-artists. All talk. All words. All empty feeling. Can't trust them. Can't depend on them. Let you down. That's for sure. Don't be taken in by con-artists.

Exploring the Word of God

In the days of Jesus, sheep and shepherds were like a family. The sheep were part of the family. They knew and trusted their shepherd. Followed him around. Where the shepherd went the sheep followed. That's what they wanted to do. They got to know the shepherd's voice. Answered his call. Trusted him.

Would the sheep answer the voice of a stranger? Would the sheep feel at home with a robber or a con-man? You can bet they wouldn't! Of course the con-man might try it on. He might even be successful on odd occasions. What a pity if he succeeded.

All the sheep had names. And the shepherd often called them by name. The sheep knew the voice. It was natural to answer and come over. The sheep got to know that the voice of the shepherd was the voice of a friend, the voice of someone who cared about them. And the shepherd's voice made them feel easy and relaxed. If someone imitated the shepherd's voice it could be a problem. The sheep might be fooled. It was a risk.

In times of danger, on dark nights, in stormy weather, it was the shepherd's soothing voice the sheep heard. When the rain was lashing down, when snowstorms were blowing, when thunder roared or lightning flashed, it was his quiet voice they heard. Or it was his strong voice they heard when hungry wolves were circling. It was his voice that meant protection and safety at all times. It made them feel good. It made them feel safe. The voice of a friend. Of course the con-man or the robber could put on a soothing voice or a strong, firm voice. Hopefully the sheep wouldn't fall for that trick. Sometimes they did. And it was bad news.

Call to Faith

We are called to follow Jesus. We are called to follow Jesus in the certainty that we can trust him. He won't let us down. We can depend on him. Always.

Call to Action

Express trust in Jesus through song. Choose a popular hymn.

Express trust in Jesus through prayer. Compose a prayer.

Express trust in Jesus by following him in the way we do deeds of generosity. Plan out some group activity that has a strong element of caring or concern.

Fifth Sunday of Easter

Gospel
A reading from the holy Gospel according to John (14:1-12)
'Do not be worried and upset,' Jesus told them, 'Believe in God and also in me. There are many rooms in my Father's house, and I am going to prepare a place for you. I would not tell you this if it were not so. And after I go and prepare a place for you, I will come back and take you to myself, so that you will be where I am. You know the way that leads to the place where I am going.

I am the way, the truth and the life; no one goes to the Father except by me. Now that you have known me,' he said to them, 'you will know my Father also, and from now on, you do know him and you have seen him.'
This is the Gospel of the Lord.

Overview
Jesus is the way, the truth and the life.
This description of Jesus is strongly philosophical and comes from the world of philosphers. This description has to do with an ideal that is set by thinkers for those who are pondering human perfection. It is far from the world children inhabit. Truth for them is about telling things as they are, at home, at school, in the neighbourhood, and not distorting the facts to save their skins, or to avoid blame or punishment.

Describing Jesus as Way, Truth and Life points to him as our goal, our aspiration, he who makes sense of our lives and struggles. In some way he is our heart's desire.

Without getting into the realm of philosophy, we can help children intuit the meaning of the Way, the Truth and Life when it is applied to Jesus. This can be done not by explaining these terms but by filling them out with images that come from the children's world.

Focusing Experiences
We want to climb that tall tree!
We want to ski that steep slope!
We want to solve that puzzle!
We want to discover the reason why!
We want to be all that we can be and more.
We want to shoot the rapids.
We want to walk a tightrope.
We want to dance like ...
We want to be a star like ...
We want to go where our imagination leads us.

Exploring the Word of God

Jesus is the Way. (Hang poster with caption: Jesus is the Way)

The way is a road, a highway, a street, a path, a track, a laneway, a tow-path, a trail. It leads somewhere. It is a guide. It keeps us right. It brings us somewhere. It leads us on. It helps us find our directions. It shows us where we are going. The way goes through swamps, forests, mountains and still leads us on.

Jesus is the Way.

We are born to look for the way.

We search for the way.

Parents help us to find the way.

Teachers point the way.

Friends urge us along the way.

It is a special sort of living.

It is a special sort of thinking.

It is a special sort of following.

We ourselves must choose to walk on that way.

Jesus is the Way. To be in friendship with Jesus is to be on the way. To be building up that friendship is to be firmly on the way.

Jesus is the Truth.

(Hang poster with caption: Jesus is the Truth)

We are always searching for the truth.

It is worth finding because it is beautiful.

It is necesasary for living.

It is necessary for loving.

We search for the truth

It is a special way of talking.

It is a way of of listening.

It is a special way of playing with friends.

We are born to search for the truth.

Parents help us in our search to find the truth.

Teachers search with us to find the truth.

Friends join with us in our efforts to discover the truth.

But it is we ourselves who have to find the truth and hold on to it. It can slip away.

We have to protect it and cherish it.

We are finding the truth when we treat people fairly.

We are finding the truth when we speak honestly.

We are finding the truth when we deal openly with people.

Jesus is the Life.
(Hang poster with caption: Jesus is the Life)
Life is running and jumping
Life is playing games and having excitement
Life is making friends
Life is talking to friends
Life is listening to friends
Life is laughing and being happy
Life is feeling joy
Life is being in a good mood
Life is having fun
Life is making friendships
Life is reading our favourite book or story
Life is watching our favourite TV programme.
Jesus is the Life. He is the best thing that could happen to us. He is happiness and joy and laughter and excitment and fun.

Call to Faith
We are called to honour and follow Jesus, the Way, the Truth and the Life.

Call to Action
Play a tape of the hymn *Lead kindly light*.
Decorate the decription of Jesus as the Way, the Truth and the Life.
Have a procession to honour him who is the Way, the Truth and the Life.

Sixth Sunday of Easter

Gospel
A reading from the holy Gospel according to John (14:15-21)
If you love me you will obey my commandments. I will ask the Father, and he will give you another Helper, who will stay with you forever. He is the Spirit who reveals the truth about God.

When I go, you will not be left all alone; I will come back to you. In a little while the world will see me no more, but you will see me; and because I live, you will also live.
This is the Gospel of the Lord.

Overview
Jesus is working for us. He will ask the Father for a Helper. The Father will give a Helper – the Spirit – who will stay with us forever.

The concept of Helper is marvellous. Children can latch on to that. It is very much part of their experience. Jesus will send a Helper – the Spirit who knows everything about God.

But Jesus' precious insight, 'because I live you also will live,' points to a continuity in relationship between Jesus and his disciples through the indwelling of the Spirit. This is deep, intangible and difficult to unravel for children.

The emphasis to-day, therefore, will be on the promised Helper – the Spirit.

Focusing Experiences
Ever act as a helper at a school concert or in Church or in the sports park?
Being helped with homework assignments.
Giving help to parents with housework.
Helped to see things differently.
Helped to achieve something when coached for our favourite sport.
Helped by way of words of encouragement. We're told we're great, that we can do it. We need that kind of help sometimes.
Helped to deal with a medical operation and a stay in hospital.
Ever feeling down? Did a pal or a parent ever help you to see the bright side of things.

Exploring the Word of God
Imagine you are disciples of Jesus. You are feeling lonely. You are feeling down. Jesus, who meant so much to you, has been crucified. Since his death, he has come among you as the Risen Jesus. But you're not sure about the future.

Imagine the Risen Jesus is among you now and talking to you. Listen to his voice as he speaks to you: 'My friends, I know how you are feeling. You feel deserted. You feel let down. You feel I have failed you. You feel I only stayed with you for a short time. Too short.

All the things we talked about – making the world a better place – spreading peace. All gone. Everything has come to a standstill. You feel nothing good will happen now. That's how you feel. I know. I see it in your sad faces. I see it in your downcast eyes.

You don't have to feel like that. I have good news for you. Help is on the way. I will send you a Helper. I promise you that . The Helper is the Spirit. The Spirit knows everything about God. The Helper will put things right. The Helper will keep us together. You and me. Keep our dreams alive. Get things moving again. I will be with you. I will be among you. The Helper will see to that. We will not be separated. The Helper wil bring us together. Together forever.

Be of good heart. Great things are about to happen. Wait for the Helper. Get ready. I bless you and love you.'

Call to Faith
Come, Holy Spirit, into our hearts, into our homes, into our lives. Bind us to Jesus in a link of love and friendship. Make us his faithful disciples.

Call to Action
Sing (choir/solo/tape) of the work of the Spirit.
Write a speech of welcome to the Holy Spirit. Warmly invite the Holy Spirit into your life, your work, your home, your concerns.

The Ascension of the Lord

Gospel

A reading from the holy Gospel according to Matthew (28:16-20)

The eleven disciples went to the hill in Galilee where Jesus had told them to go. When they saw him, they worshipped him, even though some of them doubted. Jesus drew near and said to them, 'I have been given all authority in heaven and on earth. Go, then, to all peoples everywhere and make them my disciples: baptise them in the name of the Father, the Son, and the Holy Spirit, and teach them to obey everything I have commanded you. And I will be with you always, to the end of the age.'

This is the Gospel of the Lord

Overview

The disciples are given a mission by Jesus to change the world into a good place for God.

Children can get locked into a fascination about the physical details of the Ascension. It is better to move to the heart of the Ascension message. Jesus is alive. He is the Risen Jesus. The disciples are directed to focus in on the Jesus mission to change the world into a good place for God. The directive to baptize needs to be nuanced and is best viewed on a larger canvas of changing the world into a good place for God.

Focusing Experiences

Soldiers, policemen, sailors, airmen, explorers, astronauts are sent on missions. They undertake a mission.

Students on their graduation day are given a mission.

Parents are given a mission when their child is baptized.

Husband and wife take on a mission to look after each other.

Priests take on a mission to look after their parishoners

Exploring the Word of God

Close your eyes. Jesus is speaking. Hear him. Imagine you are his disciples. Listen to his words to you:

'We planned to change the world. We are going to do it. We have a cause. We have a mission. A cause and a mission from God. We are going to make the world into a place of peace, a place where fair play will get a chance, a place where generosity will be welcome, a place where goodness will be held in honour. A new place for God. And we are going to do it.

Go out and change the world. Make the world a better place. Make the world new. Make the world a good place for God. I will be with you.

Shoulder to shoulder. By your side. Gather new disciples. Speak in the name of Jesus, in my name. And be sure that I will be with you today, to-morrow, always, to the end of time.'

Call to Faith
We are called to undertake that mission that Jesus gave his disciples, to be part of that cause – to work for Jesus, to make the world a good place for God.

Call to Action
Themes for songs and music:
    Discipleship
    The Christian vision
    Working for Jesus
    Friends of Jesus stand together
    Changing the world for Jesus
    Making all things new.

Seventh Sunday of Easter

Gospel
A reading from the holy Gospel according to John (17:1-11)
I have made you known to those you gave me out of the world. They belonged to you, and you gave them to me. They have obeyed your word, and now they know that everything you gave me comes from you. I gave them the message that you gave me, and they received it; they know that it is true that I came from you, and they believe that you sent me.

I pray for them. I do not pray for the world but for those you gave me, for they belong to you.
This is the Gospel of the Lord

Overview
In prayer, Jesus commends his disciples to the Father.
John's gospel of today is part of Jesus' great prayer for his disciples enunciated at the Last Supper. It is a rich prayer with strong allusions to the dichotomy between world and spirit.

Liturgically, the gospel marks a time of waiting and prayer before the coming of the Holy Spirit at Pentecost (next Sunday).

The richness of this gospel presents problems for children. Nevertheless, it has a prayer theme and children have a rich experience of prayer. They say their own prayers, know that people pray for them, they pray for special intentions and indeed sing some of their prayers.

Today's homily therefore presents a paraphrase of Jesus' prayer for his disciples in language for children.

The liturgical aspect, the sense of waiting and praying for the great action at Pentecost, might be marked by complementary prayers that urge the Holy Spirit to come into our lives.

Focusing Experiences
Children's own prayers. Family prayers. Prayers at Mass. Prayers at school.

Exploring the Word of God
I'd like to say a prayer for everyone here present:
'Father in Heaven, today we pray for everyone gathered in this Church. We ask you to bless us with a rich blessing of love. We ask you to keep us in your care. Watch over us at night and during the day. Be with us when we are happy and also when we are sad. Be with us when we are at peace and also when we are angry. Be with us when we are with friends and also when we are alone. Send the Holy Spirit into our hearts to make us good and faithful witnesses to Jesus.

We make this prayer in the name of Jesus, your Son, who lives and reigns for ever and ever.'

Jesus prayed for his disciples. Imagine you are present as Jesus is making his prayer. Be still, close your eyes, and listen to the prayer Jesus says for his disciples.:

'Father in Heaven, bless them. Bless all of them. They were fishermen, these disciples of mine. Boats, nets, trips to the fish markets, that was how they spent their day.

They had an eye for fish and fishing but they also had an eye for the things of God. They knew of your promise to send a Saviour, a Messiah. They waited. They waited for you to send them a sign that the Messiah was coming. Then, when I spoke the word of God to the people, they came to me as disciples because I spoke your word. They saw me as your sign in the world. They followed me and I led them in your ways.

I have given them the words you told me to give them. I have given them the wisdom you gave me for them. They know I speak in your name. They are special. They were in my keeping but they are yours. True sons of God.

Keep them in your care. Watch over them. Save them from everything that would harm them. Be with them in all their doings, all their comings and goings. Bless them with a great blessing for the work they will do for you. Be with them. Loving Father, walk with them wherever they go. Amen.'

Call to Faith
We are called to pray for our leaders among the people of God. We are called to ask God's blessing on them. We are called to ask God to bless them with love and wisdom and strength.

Call to Action
Compose a prayer for the priests in our parish.

Make a prayer asking God to send the Holy Spirit into the hearts of our priest-leaders to help them in their work with us.

Make a presentation to our priests – a gift of words (a speech), a gift of a book, a gift of gracious deeds that we covenant to undertake.

Decorate a blessing (parchment-like) for the priest.

Make a prayer asking the Holy Spirit to come into our hearts to help us to do great things for Jesus.

Pentecost Sunday

First Reading

A reading from the Acts of the Apostles (2:1-11)

When the day of Pentecost came, all the believers were gathered together in one place. Suddenly there was a noise from the sky which sounded like a strong wind blowing, and it filled the whole house where they were sitting. Then they saw what looked like tongues of fire which spread out and touched each person there. They were filled with the Holy Spirit and began to talk in other languages as the Spirit enabled them to speak. There were Jews living in Jerusalem, religious men who had come from every country in the world. When they heard this noise, a large crowd gathered. They were all excited, because each one of them heard the believers speaking in their own language. In amazement and wonder they exclaimed, 'These people who are talking like this are Galileans! How is it, then, that all of us hear them speaking in our own native languages? We are from Parthia, Media and Elam; from Mesopotamia, Judea and Cappadocia; from Pontus and Asia, from Phrygia and Pamphylia, from Egypt and the regions of Libya near Cyrene. Some of us are from Rome, both Jews and gentiles converted to Judaism, and some of us are from Crete and Arabia – yet all of us hear them speaking in our own languages about the great things that God has done!'

This is the word of the Lord.

Overview

The Spirit shook the disciples out of their lethargy. The Spirit warmed them up for their task. The Spirit filled them with a burning desire to get up and do something for Jesus. The Spirit gave them a thirst for the work of Jesus.

The first reading is full of action, full of excitement. It tells the story of the disciples who received the Spirit on that first Pentecost – rousing wind, bright fire, noise like thunder, feet rushing down the stairs into the street, cries of enthusiasm, much noise and speeches.

The first reading has to be made significant – enlarged by mime, drama, news report, interview. The first reading has to be remembered. The homily could well take place after the first reading and before the gospel.

The gospel itself should be read quietly and solemnly after some exploration of the fuss and commotion which took place in the room where the disciples were praying and in the street where they shouted out their belief in Jesus.

Focusing Experiences

Did anyone ever inspire you? Coach? Club leader? Teacher? Priest? Parent? Music or movie star ?

Did you ever watch a movie or televison story where a group of people is inspired by a leader to move, to act, to change something?

What does it mean to be inspired, to be talked into something, to be made to feel that you ought to be up and away, and into the action? What happens? What is the feeling like? Can you think back on a time when you felt inspired?

Exploring the Word of God

The disciples were calm. They were at peace. Relaxed. Then the Spirit lit them up with fire, wind and noise. Set their feelings on fire. Filled them with energy for Jesus whom they loved. Helped them to realise that they had to be out there on the streets, among the people, making the name of Jesus known. Put energy into their feet and into their voices. Gave them confidence. Made them feel that their cause was worth every ounce of energy they could give it. Made them feel good working for Jesus.

The disciples threw themselves into the task. Pleaded and argued for Jesus, explained to the people on the street what Jesus stood for. They told the people in trembling voices of the new world they could build together, the new vision, the new dream. And they spoke of the Spirit that would help neighbours and strangers to be brothers and sisters together in a great new world, in a world that would be a good place for God.

Call to Faith

Inspired by the Spirit, we are called to build a new world. We are called to love, to share, to be gentle, to be generous, to be at peace.

Call to Action

Think of slogans that would inspire the disciples to get out and speak for Jesus.

Give three reasons why you would like the Spirit to help you build a better world.

As a disciple/witness/friend of Jesus, name three projects that would be worth undertaking in your neighbourhood.

Sing songs to the Spirit.

Welcome the Spirit into your life by completing the following written invocations:

Holy Spirit, make me into ...

Holy Spirit, change me to ...

Holy Spirit , show me how to ...

Holy Spirit, guide me to ...

Proclaim the words of the gospel now.

Gospel
A reading from the holy Gospel according to John (20:19-23)
It was late that Sunday evening, and the disciples were gathered together behind locked doors, because they were afraid of the Jewish authorities. Then Jesus came and stood among them. 'Peace be with you,' he said. After saying this, he showed them his hands and his side. The disciples were filled with joy at seeing the Lord. Jesus said to them again, 'Peace be with you. As the Father sent me, so I send you.' Then he breathed on them and said, 'Receive the Holy Spirit. If you forgive people's sins, they are forgiven; if you do not forgive them, they are not forgiven.'
This is the Gospel of the Lord.

Trinity Sunday

Gospel
A reading from the holy Gospel according to John (3:16-18)
Jesus said to Nicodemus:
'For God loved the world so much that he gave his only Son, so that everyone who believes in him may not die but have eternal life. For God did not send his Son into the world to be its judge, but to be its saviour.

Whoever believes in the Son is not judged; but whoever does not believe has already been judged, because he has not believed in God's only Son.'
This is the Gospel of the Lord

Overview
Trinity Sunday is in some ways a celebration of the doctrine of the Trinity. But, rather than get involved in doctrine, it is best to help children explore the actions of the persons of the Trinity in our lives – the action of Father, the action of Son, the action of the Spirit. This approach lays the foundation for theological explorations later on.

The first reading is a tribute to God the Father 'who is full of compassion and pity'. The Second Reading is a tribute to the Father, Son and Spirit – 'the grace of the Lord Jesus Christ, the love of God and the fellowship of the Holy Spirit be with you all'. The Gospel reading is a tribute to Jesus who is God's Son.

The actions of Father, Son and Spirit are hinged on love, built on love, mediate love to us. It is through following Jesus that we link into the communion of love between Father, Son and Spirit. It is through Jesus that we meet the Father. It is through Jesus that we experience the action of the Holy Spirit in our lives.

The challenge is to find stories and words to make this communion of love real for the children

Focusing Experiences
Think of our experience of being loved (cherished, treated with affection, talked to, remembered, listened to – especially in the family)
Think of our favourite book stories, TV stories, movie stories that show love in action.

Exploring the Word of God
We remember the Trinity in many ways. Think of the shamrock. The Irish missionaries of long ago held out the shamrock to the people as a reminder of the Trinity. Three leaves, one stem.

Think of a circle. Some teachers present the circle to remind their listeners of the communion of everlasting love which the Trinity is.

Christians bless themselves in the name of the Trinity ... In some way they are joining the circle of love of the Trinity when they do this. In the name of the Father and of the Son and of the Holy Spirit. They invoke the love of the Trinity. They are calling on the love of the Trinity to touch them in some way, to be with them, to guard them.

People are exorcised from evil spirits in the name of the Trinity.

The sick are blessed in the name of the Trinity. The priest stretches out his hands over the sick person and blesses them with all the love of the Trinity.

Man and woman seal their love in marriage in the name of the Trinity which is everlasting love.

New-born babies are welcomed into the family of God's People in the name of the Trinity.

Christians bless themselves in the name of the Trinity before they begin to pray. They bless themselves to end their prayers. They like their prayer to be surrounded before and after with the sign of the Trinity.

The priest begins Mass by calling on the Trinity.

The great blessing at the end of Mass is given in the name of the Trinity. The blessing of Almighty God, Father, Son and Holy Spirit be with you all ...

Call to Faith
We are called to be part of a great community/family of love - Father, Son and Spirit.

Call to Action

Enliven the salutation :'The grace of the Lord Jesus Christ and the love of God our Father and the fellowship of the Holy Spirit be with us all.' Do it in mime. Involve everyone: Stretch out hands (The grace of the Lord Jesus Christ); Enclose arms in a circle (and the love of God our Father); Join hands with your neighbour (and the fellowship of the Holy Spirit be with us all).

Corpus Christi

Gospel

A reading from the holy Gospel according to John (6: 51-58)

I am the living bread that came down from heaven. If anyone eats this bread, he will live for ever. The bread that I will give him is my flesh, which I give so that the world may live.

This, then, is the bread that came down from heaven; it is not like the bread that your ancestors ate, but then later died. The one who eats this bread will live for ever.

This is the gospel of the Lord

Overview

The priest at Mass says: 'This is the Lamb of God. Happy are those who are called to his supper.' To hear, interpret and appreciate this declaration the children need, first of all, to have lively images of Jesus, images of Jesus from their hearing and exploring of gospel stories, images of Jesus from their prayers, images of Jesus from their visual art experiences.

Secondly, children need to think of the Eucharistic Bread as bread that is eaten by the worshipping community in a vital and sacred ritual that puts worshippers in touch with Jesus in a most immediate and real way.

Thirdly, children need to honour Jesus who is present in the Eucharist. The feast of Corpus Christi focuses our attention on the presence of Jesus in the Eucharist. We are invited to celebrate and honour that presence.

The Church has honoured and celebrated the presence of Jesus in the Eucharist, particularly through the age-old Corpus Christi procession.

The children should experience some participation in this procession today.

Exploration of the Word of God: An Action
Today's homily takes the form of a short procession in the Church. The Eucharist is carried in honour by the priest robed in decorative vestments. The Eucharistic procession is led by bearers of lights, flowers and incense. The procession makes its way around the church to the accompaniment of eucharistic songs and hymns.
Between hymns, declarations of faith (drawn from to-day's gospel) are pronounced to the people over the intercom system:
Jesus, my Lord and my God!
(Response) Feed us with the Living Bread!
Jesus, you are the Living Bread which has come down from heaven!
(Response) Feed us with the Living Bread!
Anyone who eats this bread will live for ever!
(Response) Feed us with the Living Bread!
Whoever eats this bread will draw life from Jesus, the living Bread!
(Response) Feed us with the Living Bread!
The bread that Jesus gives is his body!
(Response) Feed us with the Living Bread!
Whoever eats this bread will draw life from him!
(Response) Feed us with the Living Bread!
This is the bread come down from heaven!
(Response) Feed us with the Living Bread!
Jesus is the Living Bread!
(Response) Feed us with the Living Bread!
Come and eat the Living Bread!
(Response) Feed us with the Living Bread!
This is Jesus, the Bread of Life!
(Response) Feed us with the Living Bread!
Blessed and happy are those who are called to Jesus' supper!
(Response) Feed us with the Living Bread!

Second Sunday in Ordinary Time

Gospel

A reading from the holy Gospel according to John (1:29-34)

The next day John saw Jesus coming to him, and said, 'There is the lamb of God who takes away the sin of the world! This is the one I was talking about when I said, "A man is coming after me, but he is greater than I am, because he existed before I was born." I did not know who he would be, but I came baptising with water in order to make him known to the people of Israel.'

And John gave this testimony: 'I saw the Spirit come down like a dove from heaven and stay on him. I still did not know that he was the one, but God, who sent me to baptize with water, had said to me, "You will see the Spirit come down and stay on a man; he is the one who baptizes with the Holy Spirit." I have seen it,' said John, 'and I tell you that he is the Son of God.'

This is the Gospel of the Lord

Overview

John the Baptist is a key witness in identifying Jesus to the people as the Son of God. This is straightforward.

What might be difficult for children to appreciate is the intense interest people of the time had in these things. Everybody, just everybody, was on the look-out for the Messiah. This interest was in the people's blood, memory and consciousness. It was headline stuff all the time. Now here was someone who was pointing out the Messiah. What John the Baptist said caused ripples of excitement, of talk, of discussion, of wonderment among the people. Some people downed their tools, left their work and went to join the person John had pointed out; joined, as disciples, like the fishermen did. The Messiah and his identity was a serious matter – a matter of terrific importance to the people.

We need to capture some of this excitement in exploring this gospel story with the children.

It might be worthwhile helping the children to imagine they were there, listening to the talk and the discussion.

Exploring the Word of God

Imagine you are there listening as John the Baptist is speaking. The people are attentive to what John is saying. John is speaking quietly but convincingly: 'That's him alright. The Lamb of God! He who takes away the sins of the world! The chosen one! The Christ! You look at me in amazement. You're not taking it in. Yes, the chosen one of God. None other.

You're surprised! How can this be such news to you? I have been pointing him out all along. I told you the man from Nazareth is God's chosen one. He's the one alright. He's the one who takes away the sins of the world.

Yes, I know, I know sinners came to me and I baptized them and they felt right with God. This is different. Very different. Different, because he … he is the Chosen One. He will take away sin by the roots. He will dig deep. Dig it out. Leave no trace. I couldn't do that. I wasn't blessed by God to do that. He is the Chosen One of God. I am his servant.

He will bring us new ways of being friends with God. He will change us. He will change the world.

The Chosen One. The Chosen One of God. He is God's gift to us. We have waited down the ages for this, for him, for God's chosen one.

Can I tell you this? When I baptized him in the Jordan I saw God's Spirit come down on him. That's the truth. I saw it. I am a witness to it. God's Spirit came down on him. Marked him out. Marked him out as the Chosen One. I didn't need any more convincing. He is the Lamb of God. He is the Chosen one of God. This is a happy and blessed day for all of us. Look to him. Look to him. Our pleas to God, our prayers, are answered in him.'

Call to Faith
We are called to see Jesus as John the Baptist saw him, the Son of God, Lamb of God, our Saviour.

Call to Action
Write out some interview questions to be put to John the Baptist.
Imagine you are John the Baptist. Talk convincingly to the people about Jesus.
Write out some interview questions for the bystanders. Imagine and write out the variety of replies they give.

Third Sunday in Ordinary Time

Gospel

A reading from the holy Gospel according to Matthew (4: 12-23)

As Jesus walked along the shores of Lake Galilee, he saw two brothers who were fishermen, Simon (called Peter) and his brother Andrew, catching fish in the lake with a net. Jesus said to them, 'Come with me, and I will teach you to catch men.' At once they left their nets and went with him.

He went on and saw two other brothers, James and John, the sons of Zebedee. They were in their boat with their father Zebedee, getting their nets ready. Jesus called them, and at once they left the boat and their father, and went with him.

This is the Gospel of the Lord.

Overview

The themes of this gospel are ministry and discipleship. At the beginning of his ministry, Jesus chooses disciples. They are chosen, firstly, for their intuitive grasp of God's purpose and plan in Jesus. Secondly, they are chosen because they are motivated and driven by a deep desire to serve God. The other details of their lives - fishing skills, boats, nets, people skills are important extras, but extras.

We are talking to children. So, ministry translates into task/mission/goal/job. Discipleship translates into teamwork.

There is a further step. We are also called to be disciples. We are on the team too. We have strengths and they're needed.

Focusing Experiences

The coach, selector, manager builds the team. He considers the needs, sees who has the strengths and qualities to meet the needs, chooses his people and fills the positions.

The need is for a kicker, so a strong kicker is picked.

The need is for a defender, so a good defender is chosen.

The need is for an attacker, so an attacker with flair and ability is invited to join the team.

The need is for a runner, so a runner who really moves is chosen top of the list.

Exploring the Word of God

Jesus began to pick his team. The qualities he's looking for are clear enough. He wants men of God. Yes, men of God. People who have a feeling about God, a care for God, an ear for God, people who are able to let God into their lives, able to warm to God, able to welcome God.

He wants people who are on the look-out for God. People who like to talk about God, like to talk to God. He wants people who say that God matters to them. He wants people who have God as part of their lives.

Above all, he wants people who will jump at a chance to serve God. Who would feel good serving God. Who would put a chance to serve God before anything else in their lives. Who are waiting and hoping for such a chance.

Those fishermen knew nothing about preaching. Weren't used to speaking in public. Good with boats though. And nets. Knew how the fish ran. Could net a boatful if there was any run at all. Yes. But what has fishing to do with being picked as disciples of Jesus? Nothing much, I suppose. But fishing is about teamwork. It's about working together. It's about facing danger together. It's about being patient.

It wasn't just the fishing. Jesus saw something else in Simon, otherwise known as Peter, and his brother Andrew. He knew they'd be good on the team. Knew they'd fit in. They were men of God.

That was it. They were chosen because they were men of God. Jesus saw it in them. He needed men of God for his team.

And there was more to them. They wanted a chance to serve God. Jesus saw a way to give them a chance to serve God. Their motivation impressed him. Dedication. Yes, they had that too. Wouldn't give up easily. Wouldn't give in. Hard workers. They'd keep at it. They earned their place.

The brothers James and John were called next. They were sons of Zebedee. Their father was a bit shocked when they took off after Jesus. He didn't stand in their way, because he knew they were off to do God's work. They needed very little persuading to join Jesus' team. They wanted to become part of the team. Wanted to serve. Waited day after day for a chance like this. And now they were off with Jesus doing God's work. They were cut out for it. Happy at it.

Great fishermen all of them but even better at working for God. They had a taste for it, and an eagerness. And now was their chance. And they walked down the road together to the first village. Their work had begun.

Call to Faith
We are called to be part of Jesus' team. Chosen too. Jesus sees strengths in us. We have our own gifts that we can put to use in the team.

Call to Action
Action songs for disciples.

Songs for working with Jesus.

Prepare and do a radio interview with Simon and Andrew or James and John.

Work out a job description and a profile of the ideal candidate.

Fourth Sunday in Ordinary Time

Gospel

A reading from the holy Gospel according to Matthew 5:1-12

Happy are those who know that they are spiritually poor; the kingdom of heaven belongs to them!

Happy are those who mourn; God will comfort them!

Happy are those who are humble; they will receive what God has promised!

Happy are those whose greatest desire is to do what God requires; God will satisfy them fully!

Happy are those who are merciful to others; God will be merciful to them!

Happy are the pure in heart; they will see God!

Happy are those who work for peace; God will call them his children!

Happy are those who are persecuted because they do what God requires; the Kingdom of heaven belongs to them!

Happy are you when people insult you and persecute you and tell all kinds of evil lies against you because you are my followers. Be happy and glad, for a great reward is kept for you in heaven.

This is the Gospel of the Lord

Overview

The Beatitudes are many things. Dream, vision, guide, manual. The Beatitudes make a theme song for Jesus and his disciples as they set out on their ministry. The Beatitudes are their new way of looking at life. Gone are the legal, precise, minimalist demands of the Law. In place are the much more challenging demands of love, of humility, of mercy, of peace. The Beatitudes are rich in idea, in language, in spiritual imagery.

Children have difficulty with the Beatitudes. It might help to rephrase the (adult) language of the Bible and present the Beatitudes in language for children.

Focusing Experiences

Theme songs:

Songs for prisoners

Songs for rebels

Songs for football supporters

Brother Sun and Sister Moon was a kind of theme song for Saint Francis of Assisi. It tells of a world where everything, people and the things of nature like the sun and moon, and the animals, everything, is related to everything else like brothers and sisters.

A theme song is a way of saying something that is important to you. It's a way of saying what you hope to achieve. It's a way of saying who you are and what you are about. It's a song that becomes special for you. People connect the song with you and your group and what you stand for. It becomes your song.

People sometimes say that the Beatitudes are the theme song for Christians.

Exploring the Word of God
The Beatitudes may be presented like this:
(The following sentences are written on a chart or on a handout for the group to follow as the priest reads them and offers a short commentary)
1. Be small before God; God will make you great!
2. Go to God in your sadness; God will take away your tears.
3. Show heart to others; God will show heart to you.
4. Let others see you as you are; God will let you see the glory of God.
5. Bring peace to your friends: God will bring peace to you.
6. Work for God, even if it costs you pain and trouble; God will work for you today, tomorrow and always.

Call to Faith
The Beatitudes have to become our theme song. The challenge is a big one. But the rewards from God are big too.

Call to Action
Each listener has a written copy of the Beatitudes. Each person is invited to say to the person beside them which Beatitude they consider to be the most important and why.
Sing Beatitude songs.
Plan to do something practical and worthwhile, as a group, to show you are a Beatitude person.

Fifth Sunday in Ordinary Time

Gospel
A reading from the holy Gospel according to Matthew (5:13-16)
You are like a light for the whole world. A city built on a hill cannot be hidden. No one lights a lamp and puts it under a bowl; instead he puts it on the lampstand, where it gives light for everyone in the house. In the same way your light must shine before people, so that they will see the good things you do and praise your Father in heaven.
This is the Gospel of the Lord

Overview
Jesus speaks poetically and metaphorically. 'You are the light of the world,' he says to his disciples. It's his way of encouraging them to be a moral inspiration to those around them. With children it is worthwhile developing and enlarging Jesus' poetical imagery of light.

Focusing Experiences
Advice from parents, from teachers, from priests:
Let the light of goodness in you shine out!
Don't be afraid to let your light shine!
Let your gifts work for you!

Exploring the word of God
Light makes you feel comfortable. Darkness makes you feel uncomfortable.
Darkness creeps in around you. Light pushes back the darkness.
Light makes you feel safe. Darkness makes you feel uneasy.
In the light you find your way. In the darkness you stumble. You get lost.
Light chases away the wild animals when you are camping in the forest.
In the darkness, thieves and the like are at work.
Jesus says, 'You are the light.' You are pushing back the darkness.
You are the sun rising in the morning.
You are rays of light.
Jesus says:
'You are fireworks of light, spreading light and colour,
    shapes and patterns in the darkness.
You are light that dances in the darkness,
You are a shining star that lights up the dark night,
You are the light that comes to people in the dawn,
You are the light of a fire that brings warmth
    and comfort to those in the house.'

Call to Faith
We are called to let our light shine out.

Call to Action
Turn off all the lights in the church. Speak about light in the glow of candlelight. Look at the shadows, and patches of darkness, and the rays of light and colour all around the Church

What can be done, say, about bullying, in our neighbourhood? What can we do? What precise action can we take to discourage bullying, to prevent bullying, to make our voice heard against bullying, to let our light shine out on this issue?

And what about other things that need changing? How can we let our light shine out?

Sixth Sunday in Ordinary Time

Gospel
A reading from the holy Gospel according to Matthew (5:17-37)
You have heard that people were told in the past, 'Do not commit murder; anyone who does will be brought to trial.' But now I tell you: whoever is angry with his brother will be brought to trial, whoever calls his brother, 'You good-for-nothing!' will be brought before the Council, and whoever calls his brother a worthless fool will be in danger of going to the fire of hell. So if you are about to offer your gift to God at the altar and there you remember that your brother has something against you, leave your gift there in front of the altar, go at once and make peace with your brother, and then come back and offer your gift to God.
This is the Gospel of the Lord

Overview
You must not shout down your sister, but I say to you you must not even make a mean face at her!

This gospel reading establishes a standard for Christian morality, a bench mark. The gospel first sets out what Christian morality is not. It is not a set of laws founded on tit for tat principles. It is not just a series of commands that require us to observe or avoid certain actions – to do so much and no more.

Instead, this gospel invites us to a new level of commitment. It calls us to observe a new awareness of God and of people. It calls on us to reach out in love to people. It calls us to a new kind of thinking where we treat people not just with the minimum degree of respect but with generosity, openness and love.

We have to communicate that sense of challenge to the children. It might be best done by paralleling the gospel approach and applying this approach to children.

Focusing Experiences
Remember a time you were insulted. And a time you treated someone badly.
Remember a time you thought about revenge. And a time you deserved to be punished.
TV drama and news stories about violence and revenge.

Exploring the Word of God
If someone insults you, you can insult them back. If someone calls you

names you can call them worse names back. If someone says you are a fool, you can wait your chance and get them back. You can call them a cursed fool and a fool's fool.

If someone makes a laugh of you in the class or in the playground you can wait your chance to make a laugh of them when the time comes. And you can think about it and plan it till the thought gets black and mean in your head.

Getting your own back is a way of handling things. It's a way of living. It's a way of living with the people around you.

Jesus says it's a wrong way and a bad way. Jesus says that getting your own back – getting revenge –- really gets you nowhere. Gets you nowhere with people and it gets you nowhere with God.

He says not to trade insult for insult. He says not to call name for name. He says not to hurt with another hurt. He says not to give as good as you get. He says not to swop offence for offence. He says not to make trouble and not to bring trouble, and not to spread trouble.

He says that you, and no one else, are the one to call stop. He says you are to be the strong one. He says you are to be the patient one. He says you must stand alone if you have to. He says to put your face into the wind, bear the insult, swallow it, but don't hurl it back.

He says to bring your desire for revenge under control. He says that is the way of God. He says that is the way for a son or a daughter of God.

Call of Faith
You are called to go an extra mile, take a extra step, do an extra bit, stretch your kindness and gentleness and patience as far as it will go and even further.

Call to Action
Mime an action of insulting one another.

Write a story about getting your own back.

Change the ending of that previous story. Give it an ending that Jesus would like you to give it.

Seventh Sunday in Ordinary Time

Gospel
A reading from the holy Gospel according to Matthew (5:38-48)
You have heard that it was said, 'An eye for an eye and a tooth for a tooth.' But now I tell you: do not take revenge on someone who wrongs you. If anyone slaps you on the right cheek, let him slap your left cheek too. And if someone takes you to court to sue you for your shirt, let him have your coat as well. And if one of the occupation troops forces you to carry his pack one kilometre, carry it two kilometres. When someone asks you for something, give it to him; when someone wants to borrow something, lend it to him.
This is the Gospel of the Lord

Overview
Stories, anecdotes and wise sayings have an obvious meaning. That's one level. But stories, anecdotes and wise sayings often have a hidden meaning. Many of the things which Jesus said had hidden meanings. His audience rather enjoyed working out the hidden meaning. It was a style of communicating at that time.

We have to challenge the children to work at digging out the deeper meaning of the wise sayings we hear from Jesus.

Focusing Experiences
Collect proverbs from the group.
Examine these proverbs and discuss their deeper meaning.

Exploring the Word of God
Here's a wise saying that came from the lips of Jesus. It has a hidden meaning. 'If someone brings you before a judge in a court of law to demand your shirt, give him your coat as well.'

What can this mean? It seems a bit much. It doesn't make sense. Give your shirt and coat to someone who has hounded you and harassed you and finally landed you in court before a judge? Give him your coat with the pockets full of snakes, more likely!

What can Jesus have in mind? If man takes you to court and demands your shirt, give him your coat as well! What deep meaning does Jesus want us to hear?

Let's put his sayings into a school and home situation: If someone asks you for a pencil, give that person a pencil and an eraser as well! If someone asks you for a loan of your bike, give that person your bike for the day! If someone asks for a loan of your personal stereo, give them a loan of your tapes as well.

This is surely too much! Jesus can't be serious. No one is that generous. No one is that kind to friends. No one could put up with that kind of discomfort, of giving all the time. Or can they?

What could the story mean for us? How could it make sense for us? Is Jesus asking us to be generous in a way that is almost crazy? 'I like being generous,' you say, 'But that is surely going too far.'

Jesus wants us to go down the road of generosity farther than we've ever gone before. He wants us to be 'mad' generous, 'dead' generous, 'crazy' generous. He is asking us to be generous in a big way. That's the challenge.

Call of Faith
Don't measure out your love or your generosity or your kindness. Don't cut it into lengths and give this one so much and that one so much, depending on how they have treated you. Just be generous, be loving, be kind. Don't put it on the scales. Don't weigh it out. That's what Jesus says. Jesus says: be over-kind, be over-generous, be over-loving rather than being a Scrooge with these beautiful gifts.

Call to Action
Let's have a look at people (saints) who seem to be 'crazy' generous. Generous and loving more than anyone could or would expect.

Let's see if we can find stories of people from everyday life whose generosity, kindness or love is really on the big scale: these stories often come from situations where there is sickness, handicap, drug abuse, poverty, lack of love, abuse, etc.

Have you seen anything on TV recently? Heard any stories?

Collect proverbs from the Bible (Book of Proverbs).

Eighth Sunday in Ordinary Time

Gospel

A reading from the holy Gospel according to Matthew(6:24-34)

No one can be a slave of two masters; he will hate one and love the other; he will be loyal to one and despise the other. You cannot serve both God and money.

This is why I tell you not to be worried about the food and drink you need in order to stay alive, or about clothes for your body. After all, isn't life worth more than food? And isn't the body worth more than clothes? Look at the birds: they do not sow seeds, gather a harvest and put it in barns; yet your Father in heaven takes care of them! Aren't you worth much more than birds? Can any of you live a bit longer by worrying about it?

And why worry about clothes? Look how the wild flowers grow: they do not work or make clothes for themselves. But I tell you that not even king Solomon with all his wealth had clothes as beautiful as one of these flowers. It is God who clothes the wild grass – grass that is here today and gone tomorrow, burnt up in the oven. Won't he be all the more sure to clothe you? How little faith you have!

So do not start worrying: 'Where will my food come from? or my drink? or my clothes? (These are the things the pagans are always concerned about.) Your Father in heaven knows that you need all these things. Instead, be concerned above everything else with the Kingdom of God and with what he requires of you, and he will provide you with all these other things. So do not worry about tomorrow; it will have enough worries of its own. There is no need to add to the troubles each day brings.

This is the Gospel of the Lord

Overview

A first reading of this gospel is that God feeds and clothes the birds of the air who are free and beautiful and full of life. A first interpretation might be that people should not fret and worry about this or that - clothes and food and budget, housing and transport and insurance - God will feed them abundantly, clothe them in wonderful colours and look after them too.

But Jesus' argument is much more subtle. His argument is about being open to God's love, not getting locked into a frantic search for the good things of a material life. He is saying through this gospel story that life is also about a search for inner things, for things of the spirit – love, joy, peace, presence, pilgrimage, memory, imagination.

Focusing Experiences

Imagine this scenario: A family. They're into quality clothes. Chase after the latest styles. Watch the ads on TV. Outfits are carefully colour-matched. Like to swan around. Expensive shoes thrown in. Runners that have designer labels. A lot of talk about clothes.

Here's another family: They're into money. Endless talk about money. Kids have bags of pocket money. Plenty of spending power. Magazines, tapes, discs. Everything.

Exploring the Word of God

Are the good things in life stylish clothes, extra money to spend, good food to eat? What about the other things in life? The other things in life are the things of the spirit. It is there in that inner world that you will, particularly, be able to walk with God.

What about things of the spirit? Family time. Family outings. Working things out together. Sorting out difficulties. Listening. Talking. Consoling. Understanding. Looking out for friends and neighbours? These other things are things of the spirit, of the heart. The inside things, the deep things, things of the heart, of the spirit are nature, walking together, music, people and their concerns, prayer, thanksgiving.

Jesus says that the things of the body have to take second place to things of the spirit. Once we get into things of the spirit we are getting into the things of God. We are walking with God. We are working with God. If we make the effort to lift our attention to things of the spirit, God will be near.

Call to Faith

We are called to see beyond the world of good clothes, extra money, to the world of joy, peace, friendship where God seems particularly to dwell.

Call to Action

Songs about the world of spirit.

Write a poem about the world of nature where it is so easy to reflect on God's handiwork.

Write a poem about what friendship means to you.

Listen to beautiful music. Allow it to touch your heart. You are moving into the inner world, the world of the spirit.

Ninth Sunday in Ordinary Time

Gospel
A reading from the holy Gospel according to Matthew (7:21-27)
Not everyone who calls me, 'Lord, Lord,' will enter the Kingdom of Heaven, but only those who do what my Father in heaven wants them to do. When Judgement Day comes, many will say to me, 'Lord, Lord! In your name we spoke God's message, by your name we drove out many demons and performed many miracles!' Then I will say to them, 'I never knew you. Get away from me, you wicked people!'

So then, anyone who hears these words of mine and obeys them is like a wise man who built his house on a rock. The rain poured down, the rivers overflowed, and the wind blew hard against that house. But it did not fall, because it was built on rock.

But anyone who hears these words of mine and does not obey them is like the foolish man who built his house on sand. The rain poured down, the rivers overflowed, the wind blew hard against that house, and it fell. And what a terrible fall that was!

This is the Gospel of the Lord

Overview
The interpretation of today's gospel requires a short opening exploration of good practices in the house-building trade. Once the children have that right they can move into looking at the hidden meaning in this gospel story about good and bad building practices and how that imagery allows the imagination to consider good and bad practices in listening to the Word of God.

Focusing Experiences
Sandcastles can be very beautiful. But once the sea-tide flows in around and over them the castles are swept away, flattened and the beach washed clean of all traces of the building.

What about people who build real houses? What kind of ground should a house be built on? Sand, swamp, clay, rock?

What happens if you build a house on sand, clay, quick-sand, swamp, bogland, snow, ice? Disaster! The house either disappears, collapses, cracks, or goes lop-sided.

Why do house-builders look for a solid foundation like rock? Why do they nearly always pour in a foundation of rock-like cement on top of the clay or the sand? The weight of the walls needs something solid to rest on. Something that won't move or bend or twist or sink.

Exploring the Word of God

Listening to what God wants you to do is a bit like building.

The bad listener is like the bad builder. The bad listener listens for a bit, begins to put a few good ideas together. Some good actions begin to take shape. But the work doesn't last. The good plans and the good ideas and the good actions begin to crumble. Slowly, everything begins to float away. Not a trace left. Washed away. Not an idea left. Not a flicker. Everything goes underground, covered over. Sinks. Disappears. All those wonderful intentions. All those good plans. All those promises. Gone.

The building that is carelessly built disappears even faster if the wind blows and the rains fall. No hope at all. Cracks, crumbles and collapses like a sandcastle.

When the careless listener to the word of God is distracted in any way, suffers the least bit of pressure, every good idea, every good action about God, every good intention is quickly blacked out, forgotten, swept away, buried for good.

The good attentive listener to the word of God is like a good builder. The good builder makes a good job of it. The building is put there to stay. So does the good listener. The plans and the actions and the promises stay there. Don't come apart. Stand out clearly in the mind. Seen. Remembered. Never lost sight of. And, if the pressure is put on, the good listener can take it, stand up to it, survive it, come through with honours. God and the things to do with God are not buried or forgotten. That person gets on with doing the things of God.

Call of Faith

We are called to listen to the Word of God and act on it. If we don't give our mind and our attention to it, our efforts to follow Jesus will be lopsided, crooked and will eventually fail.

Call to Action

This building thing has to do with plans and with actions. Work out a plan of chores, for a typical ten or eleven year old, of personal choices to help brothers/ sisters, neighbours, friends. You are talking about actions that are above and beyond the call of duty in home or in school. (Doing chores without being asked).

Tenth Sunday in Ordinary Time

Gospel

A reading from the holy Gospel according to Matthew (9:9-13)

While Jesus was having a meal at Matthew's house, many tax collectors and other outcasts came and joined Jesus and the disciples at the table. Some Pharisees saw this and asked his disciples, 'Why does your master eat with such people?'

Jesus heard them and answered, 'People who are well do not need a doctor, but only those who are sick. Go and find out what is meant by the scripture that says: "It is kindness that I want, not animal sacrifices." I have not come to call respectable people, but outcasts.'

This is the Gospel of the Lord

Overview

In the days of Jesus, some people considered that they were entitled to more of God's attention and love than others. They considered themselves to be God's friends. They considered they were close to God, family with God, close relations. They considered the others, the rest of society, as outsiders. Among the outsiders that no one seemed to have a good word for were the Tax Collectors for Rome. Sinners was another name given to these outsiders.

The image the children have of sinners is of someone who commits sins, who does acts that are sinful. In the Bible the concept of sinner might best be captured by the word outsider, someone who is not considered family with God.

Jesus makes the point that what society thinks of people is not necessarily what God thinks of those same people. Jesus ate with people who were regarded as outsiders. People who didn't belong to the mainstream. Sinners they called them then.

We are all a bit weird in our own way. None of us is perfect. We don't match up. No one is entitled, because of race or custom or religion, to more of God's love than anyone else.

Focusing Experiences

Think of people who don't belong:

Outsiders

Outcasts

Those we are prejudiced against

Those who don't share our view of life

Those who seem weird for one reason or another.

Consider that the world is made up of many kinds of people. Many races. From every part of the earth. Different skin colours. Different customs. Different religions. We are all God's children.

Exploring the Word of God

Jesus was becoming a big name in the locality. Word got around. His fame was spreading. People were listening to him, discussing what he said, remembering the good ideas he talked about, thinking what they should do. Some people were joining up as his disciples. He was becoming a popular local celebrity. Very much looked up to. Respected. Lots of followers.

Some people called him a prophet, or said he was a holy man. Everyone seemed to think that he was a friend of God.

Matthew was working at his table collecting money. Some people got a bit upset when Jesus spoke to him. Matthew's job was regarded as being a bit off, a bit low, not up to much, not the kind of job that decent people would do. Matthew was working for the Romans collecting their taxes. People thought you'd have to be hard up to work for the Romans. No decent mother would allow her son to work for the Romans. Some fathers thought their sons would be better off in prison than working for the Romans. It was the way people felt. Matthew was working for that crowd and here was Jesus talking to him. That didn't go down too well. Didn't add up. It caused whispers. People complained. People even said, 'what is the holy man doing sharing talk and chat with Matthew? It's not on. We don't do the like. Someone will have to tell him that he is out of order.'

When the people saw Jesus and Matthew walk away together they were shocked. Then they heard that Matthew was chosen as a disciple. They were dumbfounded.

Worse was to happen. Jesus went to eat his dinner. He could have eaten with the headmen and the elders in the community. But what did he do? He sat down with sinners and collectors. They had no standing in the community. Didn't belong. Not the kind you mixed with. You passed them by. They weren't family. People got a bit angry and said, 'What's Jesus doing in among that crowd? He's one of us. They are not his kind. He's supposed to be a holy man. Surely he must realise that God has no time for those sort. What is Jesus up to? Why does he have to mix with them? It's so embarrassing for decent people, God-fearing people, like us. Jesus has dropped in our estimation. We thought he was great but now look what he's gone and done. He seems to have no taste'.
Jesus knew what they were thinking.

'So I am among the sinners. You could say that. I am among the collectors for Rome. I am not denying it. I am among the outsiders. Yes. The people who don't belong. Yes. I am here because God wants me to be here. Right here. Why? Because God's love is for everyone. Everyone. No exception. I have to bring God's love to the people you consider no good, who are different.

The sinners and the Collectors for Rome are loved by God too. My mission is among the people who have heart for God. My mission is among the people who are searching for God. My mission is among the people who know they need God's love. I have such people here. I am eating with them. I am sharing their company. I am bringing God's love to them.'

Many people went off home shaking their heads. They still felt that Jesus was letting himself down by talking and chatting and eating with those undesirables. They just couldn't see what sense it made offering God's love to them.

Call to Faith
We are called to receive the blessings of God's love despite our faults and our failings. We are also called to appreciate that God's love is for those who might seem to us not to deserve it.

Call to Action
Complete the following sentences:
God's love is for black (and white)
God's love is for saints (and sinners)
God's love is for rich (and poor)
God's love is for Protestant and (Catholic)
God's love is for Jew and (Gentile)
God's love is for parents and (children)
God's love is for teachers and (pupils)
God's love is for murderers and (policemen)
God's love is for men and (women)
God's love is for crooks and (honest citizens)
God's love is very beautiful.

Eleventh Sunday

Gospel
A reading from the holy Gospel according to Matthew (9:36–10:8)
As he saw the crowds, his heart was filled with pity for them, because they were worried and helpless, like sheep without a shepherd. So he said to his disciples, 'The harvest is large, but there are few workers to gather it in. Pray to the owner of the harvest that he will send out workers to gather in his harvest.'

Jesus called his twelve disciples together and gave them authority to drive out evil spirits and to heal every disease and every sickness. These are the names of the twelve apostles: first, Simon (called Peter) and his brother Andrew; James and his brother John, the sons of Zebedee; Philip and Bartholomew; Thomas and Matthew, the tax collector; James son of Alphaeus, and Thaddaeus; Simon the Patriot, and Judas Iscariot, who betrayed Jesus.

These twelve men were sent out by Jesus with the following instructions: 'Do not go to any Gentile territory or any Samaritan towns. Instead, you are to go to the lost sheep of the people of Israel. Go and preach, "The Kingdom of heaven is near!" Heal the sick, bring the dead back to life, heal those who suffer from dreaded skin-diseases, and drive out demons. You have received without paying, so give without being paid.'
This is the Gospel of the Lord

Overview
This gospel follows a flow. In the gospels of the previous Sundays we heard the vision which Jesus wanted to unfold to the world (the Beatitudes). Now comes the action. Men are to be sent on the road to spread the news, to put ideas into action.

Twelve disciples are chosen to be apostles. The 'A team' is picked. Their names are given to us. They are sent on their way.

We would like the childen to know about this team – they are linked to them in many ways. Perhaps the best approach is to talk in terms of a team being chosen for a mission. Then a close-up portrait of a few apostles – who are well known – gives a flavour of a team that we hold in high esteem.

Focusing Experiences
Do you know the names of any top sports teams? Who are your favourite stars on those teams?
What have these champions got over and above others in the sport?

What does it take to make a champion?
Did you ever have to select a team from a large list of names?

Exploring the Word of God

They were very ordinary people. Disciples of Jesus. Now chosen to be apostles.

Peter was the leader of the apostles. Great energy. Fisherman of course. Very loyal to Jesus. Great friend. Do anything for Jesus. Jumped out of a boat into deep water to get to Jesus, to be near him. Nearly drowned, poor man!

Peter had a quick temper. A bit boastful. Boasted he would die for Jesus but when Jesus was arrested Peter felt cornered. When he was questioned he denied Jesus and swore he never laid eyes on him before. Jesus forgave and forgot because he knew that Peter, despite his faults, could be trusted. He knew Peter was as solid as a rock. Jesus even gave him that name ... the rock. And what Peter did for Jesus afterwards, spreading the kingdom here and there, showed that he was a rock. Terrific leader.

Then there were James and John. Brothers. They were disciples too. And then called to be apostles. Sons of Zebedee the fisherman. Left the fishing and their father to go with Jesus. Their mother was a great woman because she took it on herself to have a word with Jesus and asked him to make her boys his top assistants, his deputies, his commanders. She asked Jesus to fit them into whatever top positions were going. Any important jobs, could they have them? Made a great speech to Jesus on behalf of her two sons.What a mother! What a good mother! Looking out for her sons. The boys must have inherited some of their mother's gift for making speeches. One day they were preaching the Word in a village in Samaria. They were not made welcome. Shown the door and told to leave. Get out of town! When they came to Jesus they were furious and said there was no reason why fire from heaven shouldn't sizzle up that mean little town. Give it what it deserved! Sock it to them! Give them a taste of lighting and thunder! Put manners on them! Needed a bit of a shock to waken them up to God's kingdom. The boys made a great speech and felt better for it. They got the nickname, 'Sons of Thunder.'

Thomas was a disciple who became an apostle. Thomas the doubter. He needed proof for everything. The others saw Jesus after his resurrection. Thomas wasn't there and wouldn't believe it. Had to see Jesus for himself. Afterwards he realised he was a nuisance. Overdoing the 'I won't believe' routine. He became a great apostle.

There was Judas. Hoped for so much from Jesus. Wanted Jesus to become a great rebel leader. Had a dream of one day being with Jesus, armed and ready to wage a guerilla war against the Romans. He was full

---

of thoughts about swords and shields and daggers. Blood had to be spilled. And he was going to be there in the thick of it. He finally realised that Jesus was a man of peace. He realised that Jesus had plans to change the world, but through love not force. Jesus would never be moved off that path. Judas was shocked by what he imagined was weakness in Jesus. For his own reasons he betrayed Jesus. It was a sad ending to a story of friendship between them both. A few days later Judas took his own life. It was the only way he could think of saying 'sorry'.

There were twelve called out from among the disciples to become apostles.

Call to Faith
In one way or another, that team of apostles went across the world and enrolled us for Jesus. They are part of what we are. We owe them respect, reverence and honour.

Call to Action
The parish 'A team' are the priests and their special helpers and ministers. We are all disciples. Could we help the 'A team'? Make it a bit easier for them. Help them out. Work with them. Be part of the great Jesus enterprise by:

Making the graveyard beautiful
Decorating the Church building
Distributing leaflets for the liturgy
Arranging flowers
Preparing colourful drawings and posters
Working with infants
Singing in the choir
Acting as Readers.

Decorate the names of the apostles. Have a liturgy in their honour.
If the name of an apostle is associated with your Parish Church, do a special celebration to honour that apostle.

Twelfth Sunday

Gospel
A reading from the holy Gospel according to Matthew (10:26-33)
So do not be afraid of people. Whatever is now covered up will be uncovered, and every secret will be made known. What I am telling you in the dark you must repeat in broad daylight, and what you have heard in private you must announce from the housetops. Do not be afraid of those who kill the body but cannot kill the soul; rather be afraid of God, who can destroy both body and soul in hell. For only a penny you can buy two sparrows, yet not one sparrow falls to the ground without your Father's consent. As for you, even the hairs of your head have all been counted. So do not be afraid; you are worth much more than many sparrows!

If anyone declares publicly that he belongs to me, I will do the same for him before my Father in heaven. But if anyone rejects me publicly, I will reject him before my Father in heaven.
This is the Gospel of the Lord

Overview
'There is no need to be afraid.' 'Do not be afraid.' This gospel is about the quality of fearlessness that Jesus' apostles must display on their mission. It is a call to moral courage, to face down opposition, to stand for the truth, not to be afraid.

With children, a good approach is to look at the way we sometimes are afraid to do things we should be doing.

Focusing Experiences
Stories and anecdotes of how someone's fear of embarrassment or shame had serious and damaging consequences.
Fear of other students in the classroom leading to wrong-doing.
Fear of punishment leading to lies.
Fear of failure leading to cheating.
We are afraid of anything that might cause friends to talk or whisper about us.
We are afraid of what people might say.
We are afraid of people laughing at us.
We are afraid of being out of fashion.
We are afraid of looking foolish.
We are afraid of looking odd.
We are afraid of being left out.
We are afraid of being jeered at.

Exploring the Word of God

'Don't be afraid,' Jesus said to his apostles. 'You'll be jeered at for doing God's work.' They had a good idea of what they were facing. The jeering. They could hear it in their imagination. The shouts, the insults, the put-downs. 'Do you hear the great scholars talking about God and they only fishermen!'

They'd be made to look foolish. They could hear the smart remarks! 'Hey, are you a prophet or something? You couldn't even tell the time of day!' 'Go home and leave the work of God to real prophets.'

They'd be told the old fashions and the old ways were the best. 'Would you look at these new kinds of priests, telling us about this upstart, Jesus. Leave us in peace. We are happy with the old ways. And here's a few rotten tomatoes to help you on your way!'

They'd be told that what they were doing made no sense. 'You're wasting your time. We don't want any talk about Jesus here, thank you very much. You're not welcome here'.

Jesus said, 'Don't give up on account of the scoffing or the cat-calls or the insults. Don't be put off. Don't be afraid. Don't lose heart. Keep going. It is the work of God you are doing. You will prevail.'

Call to Faith

Jesus says, 'Don't be afraid.'
Don't be afraid, tell the truth and face the embarrassment.
Make a stand!
Don't be put off!
Say what you have to say!
Don't be afraid to be good!
Don't be afraid to be kind!
Don't be afraid to be generous!
Don't be afraid to help the poor!
Don't be afraid to wash dishes or clean the house!
If you are a girl don't be afraid to do boys' jobs!
If you are a boy don't be afraid to do girl's jobs!
Don't be afraid to pray!
Don't be afraid to talk to God.

Call to Action

Make out a set of resolutions for the person who is not afraid to stand with Jesus, beginning with 'I promise (resolve) to do my best to...' and covering a range of everyday-life situations (moral situations that require some courage).

Collect stories about people who showed a strong degree of determination to see something through, despite obstacles and difficulties.

Thirteenth Sunday

Gospel
A reading from the holy Gospel according to Matthew (10:37-42)
Jesus said to the Twelve, 'Whoever welcomes you welcomes me; and whoever welcomes me welcomes the one who sent me. Whoever welcomes God's messenger, will share in his reward. And whoever welcomes a good man because he is good, will share in his reward. You can be sure that whoever gives even a drink of cold water to one of the least of these my followers because he is my follower, will certainly receive a reward. This is the Gospel of the Lord

Overview
We make the word of God welcome. We welcome Jesus. We welcome Jesus in the Word of God at Mass. We welcome Jesus in the priest. We welcome Jesus in our sisters and brothers. We welcome Jesus in the poor and weak.

Focusing Experiences
An experience of welcome.
Time you came home from the hospital.
Welcomed into a new school.
Welcome given to friends and relatives who visit your home.
A welcoming party.
Being made to feel unwelcome.
Stories of welcome and unwelcome from movies and TV.
What does a welcome mean? What feelings go with words of welcome?

Exploring the Word of God
Making the Word of God welcome.
At Mass the priests kisses the book of the Gospels in an act of reverence, honour and love for the Word of God. It is a welcome for Jesus who speaks his words to us. The priest says the words: 'The Lord be in my heart and on my lips as I pronounce his holy gospel.'
We welcome Jesus in our homes in the way we open our house for neighbourhood Masses, liturgies and prayer meetings.
We welcome Jesus in the way we remind ourselves of Jesus in our homes, through pictures and holy objects.
We welcome Jesus in the way our family is willing to serve in the parish as ministers and helpers to the parish community.
We welcome Jesus in the way we make the priest welcome in our homes, welcomed as an honoured guest.

We welcome Jesus in the way we open our hearts to the poor, the weak and the handicapped.

Call to Faith
We are called to welcome God's Word into our homes, through prayer and action. We are called to welcome Jesus who is God's Word.

Call to Action
Write a letter to the parish priest with some suggestions that he might find helpful.
Make an offer to help out in the parish.
Have a party for the priest in the school or club. Invite him along. Prepare speeches, songs and a small presentation.

Fourteenth Sunday

Gospel

A reading from the holy Gospel according to Matthew (11: 25-30)

At that time, Jesus said, 'Come to me, all of you who are tired from carrying heavy loads, and I will give you rest. Take my yoke and put it on you, and learn from me, because I am gentle and humble in spirit; and you will find rest. For the yoke I will give you is easy, and the load I will put on you is light.'

This is the Gospel of the Lord.

Overview

Stress is no respecter of person or age. Children suffer stress. They are sometimes in distress. They feel anxiety and experience all the attendant symptoms of stress. They need a shoulder to cry on, a listener, a comforter. Jesus is a comforter: 'Come to me you who are overburdened and I will give you rest.'

Focusing Experiences

Plenty of stories from newspapers, TV and movies about children in distress. Especially emotional distress.

Exploring the Word of God

During the past week did you feel anxious or upset?

Parents scolded you?

Teachers gave you a bad report?

Had a argument with your friends?

Felt left out?

Death of a pet?

Family upset?

Changed schools?

Sickness in the family?

Any of these distresses can hit hard and really upset us. Jesus said, 'I will be your comforter in times of distress.' We take him at his word.

Call to Faith

An invitation is offered by Jesus. 'Come to me all you who are overburdened and I will give you rest.' We are graciously invited to accept this offer of support in our troubled times.

Call to Action

What words would you use if you felt the need to talk to Jesus at a time of strain, pressure, stress, anxiety? How would you begin? How would you end?

What time would you talk? Early in the morning? At night? During lunchtime?

Where would you talk?

Fifteenth Sunday

Gospel

A reading from the holy Gospel according to Matthew (13:1-9)

That same day Jesus left the house and went to the lake-side, where he sat down to teach. The crowd that gathered round him was so large that he got into a boat and sat in it, while the crowd stood on the shore. He used parables to tell them many things.

'Once there was a man who went out to sow corn. As he scattered the seed in the field, some of it fell along the path, and the birds came and ate it up. Some of it fell on rocky ground, where there was little soil. The seeds soon sprouted, because the soil wasn't deep. But when the sun came up, it burnt the young plants; and because the roots had not grown deep enough, the plant soon dried up. Some of the seed fell among thorn bushes, which grew up and choked the plants. But some seeds fell in good soil, and the plants produced corn; some produced a hundred grains, others sixty, and others thirty.'

And Jesus concluded, 'Listen, then, if you have ears!'

This is the Gospel of the Lord

Overview

This gospel is one of a collection of parables about the kingdom. Today we hear the parable of the sower – a story of faith encountering obstacles.

In talking to children, for seed we can read friendship with God. This friendship can grow and develop. It can also flop, wither and die. Or it can stagger along for a while but never come to be anything. Or worse still it might never get a chance. It's finished before it even begins. If it is allowed to grow and develop it can become something precious and beautiful.

We are talking here of a parable. We should make every effort to tell the parable with imagination, and allow the natural texture of the words and imagery to come through. If the parable is told well it will continue to puzzle and challenge the children as they grow older.

Focusing Experiences

Putting a friendship at risk. Putting friendship at risk through jealousy, envy, meanness, lack of generosity. Taking chances with a friendship. Not working at it. Not letting it grow. Not letting it flourish.

Exploring the Word of God

He was a farmer and it was a special time. The land was prepared. The soil was soft and ready, and he was scattering the seed. He walked up the field scattering to the right and to the left. He came down scattering along a new line that matched perfectly with the previous one. He threw fistfuls here, fistfuls there. He followed a ground plan that worked perfectly year after year. If there was wind, he kept his hand and arm low and scattered gently. The wind carried the seed to where he wanted it to fall. If there was no wind, he threw the seed high into the air and it fell where it should fall. He was well practiced. He had done this season after season since he could remember. He looked around at his work. A nice even spread. No lumping. No bunching. No missed patches. No blind spots. When he finished scattering he gently raked the seed, that lay on the surface, into the soil. Covered it over. Gave it a chance to root, to settle in. Made it snug and warm. He knew that in a short time the seed would come alive and push its way out into the sunlight and begin to rise and grow. In the autumn he would have a rich golden crop.

It happened that some few seeds fell on the path at the edge of the field. There was no growing there. Solid earth, hard and trampled. The birds came and ate those seeds. No protection. Couldn't survive. The seeds that fell on the path were doomed. He was sorry because he wanted every seed to live and grow.

Some few seeds fell on rocks. They put down roots into whatever soil was trapped in the crevices and hollows of the rocks but they had a short life. He had seen it season after season. No strength. No growth. No rich earth to feed them. Withered away. Lifeless. He wished it was different. If only they could grow and flourish.

And then there was a few seeds that fell among the thorns that grew on the boundary fence. They made a fight for it. They couldn't win. The thorns were stronger and fiercer. The thorns choked them out. Blocked off the sun. Moved in and sucked out every bit of nourishment from the earth. The seeds began to droop, then withered and died quietly. No future. He wished they could outsmart the thorns, but it couldn't be. The thorns always won out.

He looked over the length and breadth of the field and knew that many seeds were already lying comfortable in the warm earth. A solid friendship. Soil and seed working together. Food, nourishment and strength to meet all their needs. The seeds would grow strong out of that rich brown earth. The seeds were already suckling the warm earth for strength and nourishment. Be able to stand strong against wind and rain. A golden harvest of growth was on the way.

Seeding time was a good time. It made him feel good. Good to be coaxing the seed, coaxing the earth, making something beautiful happen. Making life happen.

Jesus told the people to think of the seed as our friendship with God.

For some people, their friendship with God is like the seed that ended up on that path, exposed, unprotected.

For some people, their friendship with God is like the seed on the rocks struggling to survive on a hungry pocket of soil. Can't last. Doesn't work. No future. Out on a limb. The friendship with God is put at risk and the risk goes bad, fails.

For some people, their friendship with God is like the seed in the unequal battle with the thorns. Hopeless. Suicidal. Not a chance. Crazy. Should never have happened. Shouldn't have taken the risk. It was hopeless from the beginning.

For many people, their friendship with God is like the seed in the good soil. Flourishes. Does well. Stands its ground. Grows strong. People make a go of it. Things work out. They take no chances. Don't put their friendship with God at risk. Make sure to work at their friendship with God. Keep it going. Keep it growing.

Call to Faith
We are called to work at our friendship with God. Keep it fresh. We are called to avoid risks that could damage or destroy that friendshp.

Call to Action
Go on a nature walk. Discover thorns that have crowded out other growing things. Look at what happens on the path and the quality of growth you find there.
Sing songs or hymns that build up your friendship with God.
Ask the priest for a blessing to confirm you in the friendship you have with God.

Sixteenth Sunday

Gospel

A reading from the holy Gospel according to Matthew (13:24-30)
Jesus told them another parable:
The Kingdom of heaven is like this. A man sowed good seed in his field. One night, when everyone was asleep, an enemy came and sowed weeds among the wheat and went away. When the plants grew and the ears of corn began to form, then the weeds showed up. The man's servants came to him and said, 'Sir, it was good seed you sowed in your field; where did the weeds come from?' 'It was some enemy who did this,' he answered. 'Do you want us to go and pull up the weeds?' they asked him. 'No,' he answered, 'because as you gather the weeds you might pull up some of the wheat along with them. Let the wheat and the weeds both grow together until harvest. Then I will tell the harvest workers to pull up the weeds first, tie them in bundles and burn them, and then to gather in the wheat and put it in my barn.'
This is the Gospel of the Lord

Overview

This gospel is about faith surviving in hostile or evil conditions.

Children are not terribly interested in philosophical questions about evil and the freedom from divine retribution that evil-doers seem to have; they are more ready to explore the practical realities of the person who crept into a neighbour's field under cover of darkness, sowed weeds among the seeds – putting the whole crop at risk. That act can become the starting point for some discussion on evil and the threat it poses to our friendship with God.

Focusing Experiences

Any experience (TV/Movie, newspaper report) of hurt, betrayal, theft, violence. kidnap. Stories of people caught up in evil.
How are evil doers dealt with? Stories about evil doers being lynched on the spot.
Stories about evil doers being shot there and then.
Stories about evil doers living in comfort and having no apparent worries.

Exploring God's Word

It was a dark night. And it was raining. Not many people around. Most people were at home sitting around the fire. People had finished their day's work and gone off to bed and were already asleep. One man was out in the dark, very alert and very active. He was up to no good. What he was doing was evil. He crept silently into his neighbour's field and was moving around sowing weeds into the oats that were growing there. Contaminating the oats. Spoiling the oats with weeds. Why was he doing it? Who knows? Perhaps he had a grudge. Perhaps he was jealous. Could be a million reasons. He crept around during the night doing his dirty work, hiding and ducking when he heard a dog barking, or moving into the shadows when he saw a light flickering in a house. At the first sign of dawn, he was gone like an evil spirit. He had to hide and get out of sight. Didn't want to leave any clues or traces. But he left his evil handiwork behind.

After a few days, the owner of the field got the bad news that his field was contaminated. He went to see for himself. It was indeed bad news. The evil doer had done his wicked work well. Across the field of corn there was a carpet of weeds. The man of the field couldn't make sense of it. Why would anyone do this? It had to be a neighbour. A friend. A farmer like himself. He never harmed anyone. Was always a good neighbour and never did anyone a bad turn. It seemed so senseless to contaminate the corn. No rhyme or reason to it. Such waste.

Some people said he should pull out the weeds and burn them. He knew that much of the corn would get trampled in the pulling. He didn't go for that idea. In the end he told his men to leave everything to grow until the autumn. At that time he would gather everything, both weeds and corn, and separate the corn out from the weeds. He would burn the weeds in a hole in the ground. The corn he would carry back to his barns for safe-keeping and storage.

Call to Faith
We are surrounded with the possibilities of evil. We are called to hold our head high and not give in to evil. We are called to defend and protect our friendship with God.

Call to Action
If you were God how would you deal with evil doers? How would you handle them? How would sort them out? Do you think God is right to leave evil doers alone to get on with their evil deeds?

Draw a picture of evil, using colours to describe the confusion, the mix-up, the tearing apart, the upside down and topsy-turvy thing that evil is. Make up a prayer asking God to make you strong against evil.

Draw an imaginary fortress. Inside this fortress a precious treasure called 'friendship with God' is being protected and defended with all the armaments you can muster. Outside the walls various forces are making an attack. Give names to the armaments used in the defence (courage, prayer, etc) and those used in the attack (temptation, etc) .

Seventeenth Sunday

Gospel

A reading from the holy Gospel according to Matthew (13:44-46)

Jesus said to the crowds, 'The Kingdom of heaven is like this. A man happens to find a treasure hidden in a field. He covers it up again, and is so happy that he goes and sells everything he has, and then goes back and buys that field.

Also, the Kingdom of heaven is like this. A man is looking for fine pearls and when he finds one that is unusually fine, he goes and sells everything he has, and buys that pearl.'

This is the Gospel of the Lord

Overview

Finding the kingdom of heaven is getting into tune with God, getting on God's wavelength. It's about finding and appreciating the values of the kingdom – the values that are inspired by the Beatitudes, inspired by the the words of Jesus, inspired by the call of Jesus to be a worker for the kingdom. Jesus says that at the end of the day the real treasure in our lives is God and the things of God like love, beauty, wholeness and goodness. Those who search for that treasure are happy people. Those who find that treasure and keep it are blessed and blessed again.

For children the search for the kingdom of heaven might be the search for the things Jesus said were important like love – appreciating love, giving love, sharing love, and being inspired by love to do this and that at home, at school and around the neighbourhood.

Focusing Experiences

Stories about treasure. Treasure in the ground. Treasure in lost cities, in ancient tombs and monuments, treasure on the floor of the sea. Gold, silver, jewellery. We are fascinated by stories of people who hunted for and discovered lost treasure.

Stories of other other kinds of treasure that people seek, like power, like the desire to be king of the land, to become famous. Everyone has a secret dream. Everyone has a treasure that they are looking for.

Exploring the Word of God

Jesus began to talk to the people about finding God's love and beauty. It's like finding treasure he said. Treasure. Imagine finding a treasure in the field where you are working. Gold, silver, necklaces, brooches, goblets. The excitement it would be, the missed heart-beats, your eyes lighting up with excitement and wonder. Dreams of a new and wonderful life. Mind racing ahead to what all this would mean. You might have to negotiate to buy out the field where the treasure lay. You'd go to any trouble to sort it all out. No trouble too much.

God's love is a priceless treasure. If you find it, you are blessed. You are rich without equal.

Finding God's love and beauty and goodness is one thing. You have to hold on to it. You have to keep it. You have to work to hold on to it.

Or imagine seeing a pearl in the market place. You know about pearls. It seems a good one. It seems exceptional. The owner is asking a good price. You have to borrow to get the price. You have to scrounge and scrape and do without things. You have to put off other plans. But you work to buy that pearl and you buy it. It's like a dream come true. And it is priceless. It's been confirmed.

God's love is a priceless pearl. But you have to get it and to hold on to it.

Call to Faith
We are called to search for God and the things of God. And it is a valuable and precious treasure we are looking for, a treasure that makes the finders blessed for all time.

Call to Action
Write a series of sentences beginning
I get God's love at home when (my parents kiss and hug me)
I get God's love at home when ...
I get God's love at home when ...
I get God's love at school when (my friends listen to me)
I gwet God's love at school when ...
I get God's love in the neighbourhood when (my neighbours send me get-well cards).
Songs about God's love.
Write a poem about God's love.

Eighteenth Sunday

Gospel

A Reading from the holy Gospel according to Matthew (14:13-21)

That evening his disciples came to him and said, 'It's already very late, and this is a lonely place. Send the people away and let them go to the villages to buy food for themselves.' 'They don't have to leave,' answered Jesus. 'You yourselves give them something to eat!' 'All we have here are five loaves and two fish,' they replied. 'Then bring them here to me,' Jesus said. He ordered the people to sit down on the grass; then he took the five loaves and two fish, looked up to heaven, and gave thanks to God. He broke the loaves and gave them to the disciples, and the disciples gave them to the people. Everyone ate and had enough. Then the disciples took up twelve baskets full of what was left over. The number of men who ate was about five thousand, not counting the women and children.

This is the Gospel of the Lord

Overview

We have to link the feeding of the five thousand with the feeding of people at Mass.

We have to link the compassion of Jesus for the crowds who sat around hungry for food with his compassion for the hungry people at Mass who need food of the spirit.

Exploring the Word of God

Jesus sat them down and fed them. Fed five thousand on five loaves and two fishes. A miracle maybe! Extraordinary! Hard to believe! It looked like an impossibility but he did it. They couldn't get over it. A really big crowd and they all had something to eat! They were satisfied. Hunger pains went away.

Why did Jesus do it? He cared about those people, about their hunger.

What sort of picture does what he did on that day give us of Jesus? What kind of word-portrait would you put down about him? Heart of gold? Generous? Considerate? In touch with their needs? Needed no prompting? Saw what was needed? Very caring? Warm-hearted? Sensitive? Knew how they felt?

At Mass Jesus feeds us. Feeds us with the Bread of Life. The word portrait we have of him still stands for the way he feeds us at Mass. He is concerned about us. Wants the best for us.

And what does the Bread of Life that he gives us at Mass do for us? Comforts our spirit. Puts us in touch with God. Puts us in touch with God in the hope that we will work at keeping in touch with God.

Brings each one of us close to Jesus. Close, in the hope that we will stay close after Mass, in the quiet times on our own, in the other times when we are busy.

Brings our community together at Communion. Yes, together, in the hope that we will work at being together in many other ways after Mass when we go home.

Call to Faith

We are called to be fed with the Bread of Life. We are called into the presence of God. We are called into the presence of Jesus. We are called into the presence of each other. We are called to be fed with the Bread of Life. We are called to live in the new way of Jesus.

Call to Action

Compose phrases that the hungry people would have used to show their appreciation of what Jesus had done for them.

Write down what results you think Jesus would like to see coming from feeding you at Mass with the Bread of Life?

Sing a hymn or song to thank Jesus for feeding you at Mass with the Bread of Life.

Nineteenth Sunday

Gospel

A reading from the holy Gospel according to Matthew (14:22-33)

Then Jesus made the disciples get into the boat and go on ahead to the other side of the lake, while he sent the people away. After sending the people away, he went up a hill by himself to pray. When evening came, Jesus was there alone; and by this time the boat was far out on the lake, tossed about by the waves, because the wind was blowing against it.

Between three and six o'clock in the morning Jesus came to the disciples, walking on the water. When they saw him walking on the water, they were terrified. 'It's a ghost!' they said, and screamed with fear. Jesus spoke to them at once. 'Courage!' he said, 'It is I. Don't be afraid!' Then Peter spoke up. 'Lord, if it is really you, order me to come out on the water to you.' 'Come!' answered Jesus. So Peter got out of the boat and started walking on the water to Jesus. But when he noticed the strong wind, he was afraid and started to sink down in the water. 'Save me, Lord!' he cried.

At once, Jesus reached out and grabbed hold of him and said, 'How little faith you have! Why did you doubt?' They both got into the boat and the wind died down. Then the disciples in the boat worshipped Jesus. 'Truly you are the Son of God!' they exclaimed.

This is the Gospel of the Lord.

Overview

This is a marvelous gospel. The story of the disciples in a storm-tossed boat encapsulates their experiences of the comforting presence of God through Jesus Christ in moments of doubt, worry, fear or crisis. It is also a story of faith growing out of conquered fear and doubts.

Children have worries too. Jesus is a comforter. They need reassurance that the comforting presence of God is near in Jesus their friend.

Focusing Experiences

Stories and anecdotes about the experience of fear, worry, doubts. Fear of being drowned when you're in a storm. Fear of being killed by lightning when you're out in the open in a thunder storm. Fear of failure. Fear of letting yourself down. Fear of letting parents down. Fear of embarrassment. Fear of not being good enough to be a friend of Jesus.

Exploring the Word of God

Not long after the days of Jesus, his Christian community faced persecution and hardship. Christians were hunted down. Arrested. Imprisoned.

Lost their jobs. Lost their houses. Lost their land and farms. Followers of Jesus had a lot to worry about. Some of them began to lose faith in Jesus. Began to feel that maybe it wasn't worth it to be a disciple or friend of Jesus. It was such a hardship.

Christians were anxious. When they were facing hard times they often felt the need to gather together to hear the story in today's gospel. It's all about feeling fear and worry. Feeling anxious. Feeling the strain. The boat is tossed this way and that way. The disciples feel terror. Only see the deep water. See no future. No way out. Drowning maybe. Losing everything. Jesus comes to them in their fear and gives them courage. Calms things down for them. He's there with them. Reassures them. Comforts them.

The Christian community liked that story. A favourite with them when they felt menaced or threatened or helpless. Gave them courage. Gave them the feeling that Jesus was near. With them. Reassured them that it was worthwhile to be a friend of Jesus.

That story is for you too. Jesus is near when you need to be comforted. When you are worried. When you feel fear, when you are frustrated. When you are in the middle of a storm of worry. When there is a problem with your school friends. When you feel left out. When you are not sure how to cope. What to do. When there is a problem at home. A problem at school. He's there to help you, to calm the storm that's bothering you, there to help you face your fear or anxiety.

Call to Faith
We are called to remember that Jesus brings the gracious comforting of God when we are experiencing hardship or worry.

Call to Action
List the kind of fears that people of your age experience.
Write out a prayer asking for help to overcome fears or worries beginning:
   Jesus, when I feel ..., be near!
   Jesus, when I feel ..., be near!
Sing (or play a tape) of the hymn, *Lead kindly light*.

Twentieth Sunday

Gospel

A reading from the holy Gospel according to Matthew (15:21-28)

Jesus left that place and went off to the territory near the cities of Tyre and Sidon. A Canaanite woman who lived in that region came to him. 'Son of David!' she cried out, 'Have mercy on me, sir! My daughter has a demon and is in a terrible condition.' But Jesus did not say a word to her. His disciples came to him and begged him, 'Send her away! She is following us and making all this noise!' Then Jesus replied, 'I have been sent only to the lost sheep of the people of Israel.' At this the woman came and fell at his feet. 'Help me, sir!' she said. Jesus answered, 'It isn't right to take the children's food and throw it to the dogs.' 'That's true, sir,' she answered, 'but even the dogs eat the leftovers that fall from their masters' table.' So Jesus answered her, 'You are a woman of great faith! What you want will be done for you.' And at that very moment her daughter was healed.

This is the Gospel of the Lord.

Overview

Today's gospel story is a description of Jesus reaching out to strangers and foreigners. He brings God's love to a foreigner and stranger, a Canaanite woman. This story and this experience sets the tone for the Church's mission work. Missionary work today is often seen as bearing witness to our faith and our traditions among people of different faiths and different traditions. Missionaries talk about a dialogue of sincerity with Muslims. They talk about listening, about sharing, about finding common ground with people of other faiths in their different ways of knowing, loving and serving God.

Children should know about the Christian community's desire to bear witness to the name of Jesus to as wide an audience as possible. They should know about the Christian community's wish to dialogue with other great traditions. They should know that their contribution of prayer and support for missionaries and the mission effort is appreciated.

Focusing Experiences

Famous missionaries whose stories we know.

The missionaries who brought the good news of Jesus to our own land and area.

Mission magazines.

Exploring the Word of God

What is Jesus going to do? Will he speak to the Canaanite woman. Will be bring her God's love and comforting? She is a stranger, a foreigner. She is not one of the daughters of Israel. She is not one of the people who know about the prophets, about the people of God. She doesn't know the traditions or the customs of God's people. She won't know about God's plan for the people. She won't have a reverence for the God who led the people out of Egypt into a promised land. She won't know about the Sabbath and the Temple. How could a holy man like Jesus speak to her and bring her God's love and comfort? She wouldn't have a clue. God's love and comfort wouldn't be for the likes of her. Jesus would have to stay with his own because they understood better than anyone all about God and his ways.

But did Jesus hold back? Did he refuse her? Did he move out from among his own people and bring her God's love? He did, and his followers have been going to strange and foreign lands ever since, preaching and teaching and making the name of Jesus better known. The Church's missionaries are working in faraway places. In Pakistan, for instance, among the Muslim community.

Mary is a missionary sister in Pakistan. She is very friendly with local Muslim people. She is a teacher and the Muslim children have a high regard for her. She is gentle like Jesus was. She is generous like Jesus was. She is soft-spoken like Jesus was. The local Muslims think that if followers of Jesus are like that then Jesus must be a wonderful person. Mary is happy that her Muslim friends are asking questions about Jesus.

She in her turn asks questions about the Prophet Mohammed who is held in great esteem by the Muslim people. Her friends are happy that she is learning about the Muslim religion. Mary thinks that the Christians and Muslims are growing into a deeper understanding of each other's traditions. They are both growing closer to each other and to God.

Call to Faith
We are called to bear witness to Jesus at all times. We are called to bear witness to Jesus to people of other faith traditions. We are called to support our missionaries who act as spokespersons for Jesus in far-away lands.

Call to Action
Invite someone who is working as a missionary to come and talk to the group.
Find out more about Muslims. Ask a Muslim to talk to the group about the Muslim faith. Invite Muslim children and their teacher for a listening and sharing session.
Write a letter to Muslim schoolchildren in a Muslim school in a faraway land.

Twenty-First Sunday

Gospel

A reading from the holy Gospel according to Matthew (16:13-20)

Jesus went to the territory near the town of Caesarea Philippi, where he asked his disciples, 'Who do people say the Son of Man is?' 'Some say John the Baptist,' they answered. 'Others say Elijah, while others say Jeremiah or some other prophet.' 'What about you?' he asked them. 'Who do you say that I am?' Simon Peter answered, 'You are the Messiah, the Son of the living God!' 'Good for you, Simon son of John!' answered Jesus. 'For this truth did not come to you from any human being, but it was given to you directly by my Father in heaven. And so I tell you, Peter: you are a rock, and on this rock foundation I will build my church, and not even death will ever be able to overcome it. I will give you the keys of the Kingdom of heaven; what you prohibit on earth will be prohibited in heaven, and what you permit on earth will be permitted in heaven.'

This is the Gospel of the Lord

Overview

Today's gospel is about faith, faith/belief/trust/ confidence/conviction in Jesus Christ. A perfect homily might be an experience of a rousing acclamation of faith in Jesus Christ through community songs, interspersed with statements of faith in Jesus from individual members of the congregation – much emphasis on a feeling approach, less emphasis on words of explanation/insight.

Another approach would be to concentrate on the title that Peter gave to Jesus – the Christ, the anointed one. It was a title that placed Jesus in a category apart among the people. It placed him among the heroes and giants of their people, among those who had the unique distinction of being anointed – priests, prophets and kings. Christ is recognised as the anointed One ... Priest, Prophet, King. It marked him out as God's anointed. It was a title of very great significance among the people. He was singled out as God's man, Son of God, worthy of our admiration, our trust, our faith.

Focusing Experiences

Heroes from popular culture.

Heroes from our myths and legends.

Heroes from our history.

Heroes in our traditions who inspired and led the community to great things.

Heroes in our traditions who led us as God's people.

Heroes in our community whose words and wisdom and sayings are remembered and revered.

Exploring the Word of God
Our forefathers in the faith, the Jews, had a special reverence for their prophet, their priest and their king. Prophet, priest and king were anointed into their jobs. Prophet, priest and king were very important people. Highly regarded in the community. Centre of the community. The heart of the community. The people knew that the hand of God was on these great leaders to bless them and support them in their work. The people looked to them for wisdom, for advice, for help. The people followed their priest, their prophet and their king.

Hero kings: the people followed them wherever they led, even to death.
Hero priests: their words of wisdom about God were listened to with great respect. Priests were leaders of worship and leaders of prayer.
Hero prophets: their advice, their strong words, their stinging criticisms were accepted because they spoke out for God.

When Peter acclaimed Jesus as the Christ, the anointed one, he was paying Jesus a very great compliment. He was paying him a great honour. He was singling him out as a hero among God's people. He was declaring that he was one with the priests, prophets and kings. A singular honour. A recognition that he was the man of God among the people. There was a hush among the disciples when Peter spoke like this about Jesus. Peter was saying that we could, with full heart, have faith and belief in Jesus as God's man among us. It was a tremendous vote of confidence in Jesus. It was a vote of faith in Jesus.

Call to Faith
Jesus, you are the voice and presence of God among us. We honour you. We believe you. We put our trust in you. We are ready to follow you. Lead us into new ways of loving God.

Call to Action
Songs of praise for Jesus.
Community songs of faith.
'One line' personal declarations of faith in Jesus from the congregation.
'One line' personal histories of faith in Jesus, especially from parents and more senior members of the community.
Resolutions to express our faith in Jesus in family settings (at night perhaps).

Twenty-Second Sunday

Gospel
A reading from the holy Gospel according to Matthew (16:21-27)
From that time on Jesus began to say plainly to his disciples, 'I must go to Jerusalem and suffer much from the elders, the chief priests, and the teachers of the Law. I will be put to death, but three days later I will be raised to life.' Peter took him aside and began to rebuke him. 'God forbid it, Lord!' he said. 'That must never happen to you!' Jesus turned around and said to Peter, 'Get away from me, Satan! You are an obstacle in my way, because these thoughts of yours don't come from God, but from man.' Then Jesus said to his disciples, 'If anyone wants to come with me, he must forget self, carry his cross, and follow me.'
This is the Gospel of the Lord.

Overview
There is a down side to following Christ. A pain side. An uncomfortable side. There is struggling to be done and obstacles to be overcome. Every so often we have to check ourselves and call ourselves to order. We have to renew our direction and look again towards our goals.

Following Jesus brings satisfaction, but is not without tough decisions and a little pain and discomfort. Jesus' call to love can fall on our deaf ears. The call to peace can be lost in the noise of argument, confrontation and aggression.

We have to tell children about the joy and about the stuggle, about the successes and the failures, about the ups and downs of Christian living.

Focusing Experiences
Explore the experience of enjoying a friendship, yet recognising that there has to be discomfort. There has to be a struggle against obstacles, misunderstandings, differences of opinion if the friendship is to be satisfying for both sides.

Discuss the joy and satisfaction of our relationship with parents and yet the discomfort and hard decisions needed to make things work out for the whole family. Sometimes we have to give ground, make concessions, show extra understanding, give up privileges, put off pleasures for the sake of good harmony among all the family members. And it's a pain! Real discomfort.

Explore the the satisfaction of being in a club or team. Yet there are times we have to struggle with ourselves to really listen to what others are saying and what others are feeling if we are to make the club work for us and everyone in it.

Exploring the word of God

Jesus said: There is pain, difficulty and struggle in following me. Deal with the tough times! Don't run from the pain! Don't avoid the discipline! Don't hide from the discomfort! Face it! And you will have life.

Some people pass up on the challenge. That can be a great pity. Perhaps they are afraid of the discomfort. Maybe they are not used to discomfort. It is much easier to roll with the tide. Maybe the easy way out seems a better deal to them.

To become strong in spirit ourselves, we need to be able to suffer discomfort.

To build friendship we need to be able to suffer discomfort.

To be an effective part of the group we need to be able to suffer discomfort.

Call to Faith

We are called to walk a path of glory with Jesus. Jesus invites us to walk that path with him as his followers but alerts us that the path has some rough stones and some sharp thorns.

Call to Action

Revive memories of action stories of saints and sinners who struggled, who faced the challenge, who faced the discomfort and followed Jesus ... hermits, nuns, monks, prisoners, parents, children.

Think aloud of the isolation and suffering Jesus himself faced.

Engage in some form of discipline or discomfort to achieve a worthwhile goal. Do a short fast to be at one with those millions of our brothers and sisters who are starving. Do chores at home that require a full day's commitment. Do gardening for a neighbour who is incapacitated in some way.

Draw a black, bleak picture of the cross of Christ, the great reminder of the pain of following Jesus. Bathe it in rich, bright colours of resurrection to remind us of the glory that comes after the suffering of the cross.

Twenty-Third Sunday

Gospel
A reading from the holy Gospel according to Matthew (18:15-20)
Jesus said to his disciples, 'If your brother sins against you, go to him and show him his fault. But do it privately, just between yourselves. If he listens to you, you have won your brother back. But if he will not listen to you, take one or two other persons with you, so that "every accusation may be upheld by two or more witnesses," as the scripture says. And if he will not listen to them, then tell the whole thing to the church. Finally, if he will not listen to the church, treat him as though he were a pagan or a tax collector.'
'And so I tell all of you: what you prohibit on earth will be prohibited in heaven, and what you permit on earth will be permitted in heaven. And I tell you more: whenever two of you on earth agree about anything you pray for, it will be done for you by my Father in heaven. For where two or three come together in my name, I am there with them.'
This is the Gospel of the Lord.

Overview
This gospel is about community, the focused power of the community.

We belong to God's people. That people operates not as individuals, with all their different agendas, but as a community. The community takes on a life of its own, empowering, forgiving, reconciling the individuals who belong to its network of common concerns.

It is a good idea to help the children to a sense of what community is and means. A powerful homily could take the form of a ritualised expression of community building (thanking God for local community strengths) or a ritualised expression of community reconciliation (Penance service). On the other hand, an exploration of community values and concerns might be equally effective.

Focusing Experiences
Experiences and stories of community activities (activities that generated a sense of community, a sense of the group working together for the common good, a sense of belonging, a sense of fellowship, a sense of tradition).
Experiences of community concerns and difficulties
(building development, traffic congestion, school availability, library facilities, road dangers, street safety, shopping facilities, litter problems, graffiti).
Experience of community reconciliation. Getting together of Catholic, Protestant and Jew, or blacks and whites.

Experiences in the family, school, neighbourhood, the wider environment.

Exploring the Word of God
Our Christian community assembles together. We come from many homes to one place of meeting. There is a feeling of strength, of solidarity in the assembly. We are, all together, a great extended family.

We pray together as a community. The priest leads the community in its prayer. When we are together, we ask forgiveness of each other. We sing together. We sing hymns of praise to God with one voice. In community, we are a strength, a power. A great family of many voices, many gifts and talents.

Jesus says the community is a power for good. Jesus says the community has a strength to heal and forgive. Jesus says the community must be alive and well and strong to act as a force for good. Jesus says we should grow in community and act in community.

Call to Faith
We are called to be a community of Christ's followers. We are called to act as a community, to grow together as a community, to be a source of strength for each other in this community.

Call to Action
Arrange a community act of community-building and reconciliation in Church.
Plan a family act of family-building and reconciliation around the table at home.
Devise a school assembly of community-building and reconciliation in the school hall.
Gather as a community and talk to God in prayer.
Sing songs and hymns that are community-centred.

Twenty-Fourth Sunday

Gospel

A reading from the holy Gospel according to Matthew (18:21-35)

Peter came to Jesus and asked, 'Lord, if my brother keeps on sinning against me, how many times do I have to forgive him? Seven times?' 'No, not seven times,' answered Jesus, ' but seventy times seven, because the kingdom of heaven is like this. Once there was a king who decided to check upon his servants' accounts. He had just begun to do so when one of them was brought in who owed him millions of pounds. The servant did not have enough to pay his debt, so the king ordered him to be sold as a slave, with his wife and his children and all that he had, in order to pay the debt. The servant fell on his knees before the king, "Be patient with me and I will pay you everything!" The king felt sorry for him, so he forgave him the debt and he let him go. Then the man went out and met one of his fellow-servants who owed him a few pounds. He grabbed him and started choking him. "Pay back what you owe me!" His fellow-servant fell down and begged him, "Be patient with me and I will pay you back!" But he refused. Instead he had him thrown into jail until he should pay the debt. When the other servants saw what had happened, they were very upset and went to the king and told him everything. So he called the servant in. "You worthless slave! I forgave you the whole amount you owed me, just because you asked me to. You should have had mercy on your fellow-servant, just as I has mercy on you." The king was very angry, and he sent the servant to jail to be punished until he should pay back the whole amount.' And Jesus concluded, 'That is how my Father in heaven will treat every one of you unless you forgive your brother from your heart.'

This is the Gospel of the Lord

Overview

Today's gospel is about forgiveness. Jesus sets no limits on forgiveness. He asks his followers to be boundlessly generous in forgiving.

We have to help children to explore forgiveness. We can extend their personal experience through story and anecdote. It is important to remember that children feel very deeply. Their feelings of anger or frustration or upset can be very deeply felt and the movement towards forgiveness can only be expected when those feelings have subsided somewhat.

Focusing Experiences

Explore personal experiences of being forgiven at home in the family. Recall personal experiences of giving forgiveness to those who have offended us – brothers or sisters or friends.

Encourage people to remember stories of forgiveness that made a strong impact on them, stories read in books or seen on TV.

Words of forgiveness: 'It's ok.' 'Don't worry.' 'I forgive you.' 'I want to forget about this.' 'I'm not mad anymore.' 'I was feeling hurt. I'm not feeling hurt anymore.'

Exploring the Word of God

Forgiveness comes from someone whose feelings have been hurt, or who has been upset, or who has been put down, or made to feel small. What does it mean to be hurt or wronged? What does it mean to have one's rights violated? What does it mean to have one's feelings trampled on? First you feel anger and annoyance towards the person that hurts you. Then you can feel hate. Maybe loathing. Maybe bitterness.

In forgiveness you don't feel hate anymore. You don't feel anger anymore. You don't feel bitterness anymore. You feel at peace. You are able to give the gift of forgiveness to whoever has hurt you. It's a big thing to do. It's a great temptation to hold on to the hurt and let it grow.

Jesus says that giving the gift of forgiveness is a very beautiful thing.

Jesus tells a lovely story of forgiveness. In the story that Jesus told, you have a king who is generous and forgiving, and a servant who is mean and unforgiving. The king says to the man he forgives, 'Forget it. It's ok. Don't worry about it. It's alright. We won't say anything more about it. It's nothing. We start again. New beginning. A clean page. It will never be mentioned. No, I don't want you to thank me. I just want to let by-gones be bygones. What happened yesterday or last week is over and done with. Today is a new day. No, please I must insist that we never as much as mention this subject again. It's done. It's finished with. It's buried. It's over. Don't go on and on about it. I said this business between us is settled and finshed. Forgotten. I really mean that. I won't even think about it ever again. It's a closed book. Agreed?'

And the unforgiving servant ... this is how he comes out in Jesus' story ... this is the kind he is ... this is the way he speaks: 'I don't forget anything. I don't forgive anything. I'll remember this against you until you go into your grave. I'll get my own back and with interest. What you did you did and I'll make sure you pay for it. I won't let you forget it. And don't think you can slide away from what you owe me. I won't let you breathe until I get my own back. I'll persecute you every day of your life. Forgiveness! No way! I'm not a fool. I'm not soft. I want what I want and I'll get it. Is that clear? I'll make you pay dearly for what you have done.'

In the story the unforgiving servant is a big loser in the end. Jesus is saying that unforgiving people are losers in the end.

Why is that so? Maybe because the hurt keeps gnawing at them. The hurt keeps them from growing in love. Keeps them chained in some way. Ties them down. Keeps their spirit small. Keeps them from growing in love.

Call to Faith
We are called by Jesus to forgive, not once or twice, but seven times. And not just seven times but seventy times seven times. And not just seventy times seven times, but to keep on forgiving and forgiving.

Call to Action
Mime gestures of forgiveness.
Write out phrases of forgiveness.
Dramatise a forgiveness scene.
Write a story about forgiveness.
Compose prayers asking God's forgiveness.
Arrange for a community forgiveness service.

Twenty-Fifth Sunday

Gospel
A reading from the holy Gospel according to Matthew (20:1-16)
Jesus said to his disciples, 'The Kingdom of God is like this: Once there was a man who went out early in the morning to hire some men to work in his vineyard. He agreed to pay them the regular wage, a silver coin a day, and sent them to work in his vineyard. He went out again to the marketplace at nine o'clock and saw some men standing there doing nothing, so he told them, "You also go and work in the vineyard, and I will pay you a fair wage." So they went. Then at twelve o'clock and again at three o'clock he did the same thing. It was nearly five o'clock when he went to the marketplace and saw some other men still standing there. "Why are you wasting the whole day here doing nothing?" he asked them. "No one hired us," they answered. "Well, then, you also go and work in the vineyard," he told them.

When evening came, the owner told his foreman, "Call the workers and pay them their wages, starting with those who were hired last and ending with those who were hired first." The men who had begun to work at five o'clock were paid a silver coin each. So when the men who were the first to be hired came to be paid, they thought they would get more; but they too were given a silver coin each. They took their money and started grumbling against the employer. "These men who were hired last worked only one hour," they said, "while we put up with a whole day's work in the hot sun – yet you paid them the same as you paid us!"

"Listen, friend," the owner answered one of them, "I have not cheated you. After all, you agreed to do a day's work for a silver coin. Now take your pay and go home. I want to give this man who was hired last as much as I have given you. Don't I have the right to do as I wish with my own money? Or are you jealous because I am generous?"'

And Jesus concluded, 'So those who are last will be first, and those who are first will be last.'

This is the Gospel of the Lord.

Overview

This gospel is about God's generosity. God's generosity doesn't make business sense. It doesn't make any real sense to us who measure things out in portions according to certain calculations related to effort, energy expended, output achieved. We pay wages in return for work. We often pay by the hour. It's clear-cut and business-like. Wages have to be related to profit. We live in a world of accountants and calculators. We live by profit and loss.

God lives by love. God is love. God is in a different league from us when it comes to sharing out love. No petty calculations. No measuring out, measure by measure. It's not God's way at all. God is always over the top. Always way out in his generosity. Always loving to excess.

Children enjoy this story that Jesus told because they have a keen sense of justice. And at first reading the story seems to offend their sense of justice, of fair play. They get het-up about the workers who got a full day's wages and yet only did a hour's work. It creates an interesting backdrop to our explanations about God's inexplicable and extraordinary generosity.

Exploring the Word of God

Jesus told the story in a straightforward way. People came and worked in this particular place. Some of them worked for an hour. Some for two hours. Some for three hours. Some for six hours. For the whole day even.

When they came to be paid, they were all paid the same wages, the same money. Everyone got a full day's wages. The full amount. Not a penny held back. Paid in full. Everybody. That was a strange thing. The person who worked for one hour got a full day's wages, the same wages as the person who worked the whole day. The person who worked for two hours got a whole day's pay, the same money as the person who worked for six hours. When they heard this story, people looked at each other in amazement. What kind of a boss was this. Crazy? Did he have any business sense at all? Could he not do sums? How could someone who worked for a part of an hour be entitled to a full day's wages? It didn't add up. It didn't make any sense. It didn't make any business sense.

In the days of Jesus, stories were a popular way of discussing the issues of the day. Stories were listened to carefully and discussed. Stories were the question-time and the quizz-shows and the crossword-puzzles of the day. People enjoyed stories. They expected to have to work on a story, sort it out, get their teeth into it. They expected to have to look for a meaning. This story that Jesus told really had them talking.

Just imagine. Say you go and do babysitting (or gardening) for an hour. Someone else does it for two hours, someone else for a whole day. And you all get a full day's pay for your trouble, whether it was an hour, two hours or a whole day. Full wages. It seems over the top. It's too generous.

What can Jesus be getting at in his story? Who is this boss who is paying the full day's wages to everyone. Who is this person whose generosity is out of the ordinary, whose generosity doesn't make any business sense, who breaks the rules of what we think is common sense?

What is Jesus saying about God? What is he saying about the way God pays out his love? That's what the story is about.

Call to Faith
We are called to receive God's love. That love is not paid out, measure by measure, as we earn it, but with a generosity that is astounding. God's generosity is not like human generosity.

God's love flows powerfully to all. It is not marked or measured. It just keeps coming. God is like that with us. God has no sense when he is dealing with us!

Call to Action
Songs of praise for God who is generous to a fault.
Songs about God's love.

Twenty-Sixth Sunday

Gospel

A reading from the holy Gospel according to Matthew(21:28-32)

Jesus said, 'Now, what do you think? There was once a man who had two sons. He went to the older one and said, 'Son, go and work in the vineyards today.' 'I don't want to,' he answered, but later he changed his mind and went. Then the father went to the other son and said the same thing. 'Yes sir,' he answered, but he did not go. Which one of the two did what the father wanted?'

'The older one,' they answered.

So Jesus said to them, 'I tell you, the tax collectors and prostitutes are going into the kingdom of God ahead of you. For John the Baptist came to you showing you the right path to take, and you would not believe him; but the tax collectors and the prostitutes believed him. Even when you saw this, you did not later change your minds and believe him.'

This is the Gospel of the Lord.

Overview

The gospel of today is an age-old story that would fit any time, any culture. It's a story that we can feed on, ponder, take sides on. In the context of the people to whom Jesus told the story there were some obvious connections. One could draw this connection: the Pharisees gave centuries of service and commitment to the Lord. It looked like they might go the final step with Jesus. They seemed all set to follow God's Messiah. But they refused.

The outsiders – those who were not among the chosen – at first refused to walk with God, but they changed their mind and found God in Jesus. These kinds of connections might be too remote for children. There are other connections.

The children should be encouraged to let this story work its own kind of magic on their imagination. The first task of the preacher is to bring this story alive by expanding it and telling it in a lively way. Putting the children in touch with this story, and helping them to explore it as a story for today, might bring worthwhile rewards.

Focusing Experiences

What do these sentences mean to you?

What kind of people do you think we are talking about?

When would you say these things about people?

She is a woman of her word.

He keeps his word.

My word is my bond!

I've given my word.

I won't break my word.

What do these sentences mean to you?

What kind of people do you think we talking about?

When would people make these statements?

I've changed my mind.

I see things differently now.

I have realised something.

I now see the light.

I got it wrong.

I came to my senses

I was stupid.

I wasn't really thinking then. Now it's different.

Exploring the Word of God

The father spoke to his two sons, 'Go down to the vineyard and do a day's work,' he said to both of them. One son, a difficult, troublesome lad, said he wouldn't go. Definitely wouldn't go. That was that. He wouldn't go. But things can and do change. That son thought about his refusal. He decided that he was in the wrong. He changed his mind and went down to the vineyard and did what his father asked him to do.

The other son, a good lad who never seemed to put a foot wrong, heard what his father asked. He heard his father say, 'Go down to the vineyard and do a day's work.' His answer was: 'Of course I'll go. I'd be glad to go. I want to help out. No trouble at all. I'm on my way. Leave it with me.' But after all these fine promises, he did't go. He never went near vine or vineyard. He just made up his mind he wouldn't go. And he never went. It was a pity.

Which son would you praise? Which son would you have the good word for? Which son would impress you?

Well there was that first son, the troublesome lad; at first he refused to go. No marks for that. He turned his father down. That deserves no praise. That was bad. We have tell him out straight that what he did was wrong. But then he changed his mind. He saw he was wrong. He saw he was out of order. He admitted his mistake to himself. He decided to put things right. He said to himself. 'My father asked me go down to the vineyard and do a day's work. I know I refused. Well, I'm changing my mind. Now I'm going. I'm on my way.' He went down to the vineyard and did a mighty day's work. It was a fine day's work and he was glad he did it.

He definitely deserves a lot of praise. We have to admire him for the way he changed his mind. We have to admire him for the way he came good in the end. We have to admire him for the way he came around.

118

The other son, who never seemed to put a foot wrong, said he would go. He didn't even have to take time to consider. He said he was delighted to go. As far as one could gather from his words and the way he nodded his head, he was all set to go. He even repeated that he was looking forward to going. But he didn't go. Maybe he had the good intention. We'll never know. He didn't move next or near the place. Now that's a mystery. Was he a hyprocrite? Was he a bluffer? Saying one thing and meaning another! It's hard to figure him out. What on earth got into him? Who did he think he was conning? It was a shame that he couldn't be a man of his word. We can't give him any marks for what he did. His words were empty. Just words. He stayed where he was and didn't go. He let his father down. Worst of all, he let himself down.

Call of Faith
You have turned you back on Jesus sometimes. You are called to change your mind, change your ways, find your feet and follow Jesus.

Call to Action
Try to find words and sentences for people who are sinners and come back to God.
- a returned sinner.
- a sorry sinner.
- a repentant sinner.

Do you know any stories of people who changed their ways? Imagine one and write it down.

Have you any favourite bible stories about sinners who changed their minds and came to God? In the story of Zacchaeus, or the Prodigal Son, what part do you like best?

Twenty-Seventh Sunday

Gospel
A reading from the holy Gospel according to Matthew (21:33-43)
'Listen to another parable,' Jesus said. 'There was once a landowner who planted a vineyard, put a fence around it, dug a hole for the winepress, and built a watch-tower. Then he let out the vineyard to tenants and went on a journey. When the time came to gather the grapes, he sent his slaves to the tenants to receive his share of the harvest. The tenants siezed his slaves, beat one, killed another and stoned another. Again the man sent other slaves, more than the first time, and the tenants treated them the same way. Last of all he sent his son to them. 'Surely they will

---

respect my son,' he said. But when the tenants saw the son, they said to themselves, 'This is the landowner's son. Come on, let's kill him, and we will get his property!' So they seized him, threw him out of the vineyard, and killed him. 'Now, when the owner of the vineyard comes, what will he do to those tenants?' Jesus asked. 'He will certainly kill those evil men,' they answered, 'and let the vineyard out to other tenants, who will give him his share of the harvest at the right time.' Jesus said to them, 'Haven't you ever read what the Scriptures say? The stone which the builders rejected as worthless turned out to be the most important of all. This was done by the Lord; What a wonderful sight it is!'

'And so I tell you,' added Jesus, 'the Kingdom of God will be taken away from you and given to a people who will produce the proper fruits.' This is the Gospel of the Lord.

Overview
A great story. There is a temptation to pass quickly over stories like this to get to the point. That would be a pity. If this story gets well settled into the children's imagination, it will grow with them through the years. We have a real obligation to tell Jesus' stories well, especially when the children's imagination is so hungry for action.

Focusing Experiences
Claim jumping.
Sheep or cattle rustling.
Violent coups that remove legal Heads of State

Exploring the Word of God
In the days of Jesus, some people thought they would take over God's kingdom and run it their way. The way Jesus saw it, God would be left out of things and these interlopers would decide what was best for everybody. They would speak for God. They would decide what God wanted. They would be the voice of God. Jesus told them a story about a vineyard to warn them that God wouldn't let them take over God's kingdom to run it their way.

It was a pleasure to look at the place. And people did. They admired the strong vines, the healthy leaves and the great bunches of grapes on every vine. There was a wall around the vineyard, a stone wall, very neat, very strong. It gave a finished look to the vineyard. Just behind the wall and near the long row of vines was the wine press. It was natural that the wine produced there soon got a reputation for quality.

The people who tended the vineyard for the owner were the tenants. They knew a lot about vines and a lot about wine. They were well paid for their work. Free wine for them, and a certain amount of the profit from the sale of the wine (which actually sold very well). Harvest time was money time for all those connected with the vineyard. The tenants got their share and the owner sent messengers to bring back his share. This arrangement worked really well for a while. Then the tenants got greedy. When the messengers came for the owner's share, they were roughed up and sent back to the owner in bad shape. The tenants really had an eye on the vineyard for themselves. The owner didn't give up that easily. When the next season came around, he again sent messengers to collect his share of the profits. But he sent more messengers this time. The extra numbers would make a difference, he thought. But it made no difference. This time the tenants were really vicious. They used knives, cudgels and stones to slash and injure the messengers. When the attack was over one of the messengers lay dead. Another had his head opened with a stone.

The owner couldn't believe this bad news and gave it a lot of thought. When the time came around again to send for his share he had a plan all ready. He would send his son. The tenants wouldn't be brazen enough to lay a finger on his son. They would respect his son, listen to him and fulfill their part of the bargain. Off the son went to meet the tenants and talk sense to them. The tenants recognised him as soon as they saw him. 'That's the son,' they said. 'We know the law of the land. If the son were to die we would inherit the vineyard. It would have to come to us.'

They decided to murder the son and inherit the vinyard. They got a plan ready. They crowded in on the son. Rushed him. Gave him no chance. Cut him down. Finished him off.

When the owner heard the news of his son's murder, he gathered a force and wasted no time tracking down the murderers. Every last one of them was cleared out of the vineyard and every last one of them got what they deserved. Eventually the vineyard was given over to other tenants who worked well with the owner.

Call to Faith
We are the tenants in God's vineyard. We are called to work with God. Not work against God. We are called to make the vineyard good for God not good for us. We do this work with Jesus, who leads the way. If we are selfish, we lose the vineyard.

Call to Action
Renew your commitment to be workers in God's kingdom.
Sing a hymn/song for Workers in God's kingdom.
Take cuttings from local papers to highlight local injustices.
Focus on some of the great workers in God's kingdom.
Have a sensitivity time for people who are disabled. Invite speakers from local groups.

Twenty-Eighth Sunday

Gospel

A reading from the holy Gospel according to Matthew (22:1-14)

Jesus again used parables in talking to the people. 'The kingdom of heaven is like this. Once there was a king who prepared a wedding feast for his son. He sent his servants to tell the invited guests to come to the feast, but they did not want to come. So he sent other servants with this message for the guests: "My feast is ready now; my bullocks and prize calves have been butchered, and everything is ready. Come to the wedding feast!" But the invited guests paid no attention and went about their business: one went to his farm, another to his shop, while others grabbed the servants, beat them, and killed them. The king was very angry; so he sent his soldiers, who killed those murderers and burnt down their city. Then he called his servants and said to them, "My wedding feast is ready, but the people I invited did not deserve it. Now go to the main streets and invite to the feast as many people as you find." So the servants went out into the streets and gathered all the people they could find, good and bad alike; and the wedding hall was filled with people.'

This is the Gospel of the Lord.

Overview

This story has strong connections with God's people, the people of Israel, who are implored by Jesus not to miss the Wedding Feast with God, not to miss their appointment of destiny with the God who loves them. Not to miss the Messiah. Not to dismiss the voice of God ringing in their ears through the saving words of Jesus.

It has connections with the children too, who are invited to respond to God's invitation to come into the feast of God's friendship. A response of deeds and actions is required

Focusing Experiences

Invitations to weddings, birthdays and other celebrations:

The feelings behind an invitation. When you are invited to a birthday party you are being invited into a deeper friendship with the person who invites you. There's more to it than eating cakes. It's about sharing, feeling good about your friends, wanting to have your friends around you on the special occasion. It's about wanting to celebrate with those you really care about.

Feelings experienced when a wedding or birthday invitation is refused. There's a hurt, a sense of loss. You feel you're going to miss your friend's companionship and support.

122

Exploring the Word of God

It was no ordinary wedding. It was no ordinary invitation. It was the wedding of the King's son and the invitation was from the king. Invitations were sent far and wide to the great people of the land. 'Come to the feast,' it read, your king invites you to the feast. Now an extraordinary thing happened. Nobody wanted to come to the wedding feast. Nobody knows why there was so little interest. But it was a fact that the king didn't get a single reply. Nobody, just nobody wanted to come.

'There is some mistake,' said the king, 'some misunderstanding. Some problem. It's nothing that can't be overcome and sorted out. I have a new plan that will clear up the matter.' He assembled his messengers and instructed them to go to those who were invited. 'Tell them,' he said, 'that everything is ready; the food, the music, the entertainment. Tell them to hurry and come. The feast is ready.'

The king waited for the replies, expecting to hear from people up North, down South, over in the East and across in the West. He heard nothing. Not a single reply. It was clear that those who were invited weren't coming. When he enquired further he was told that the invited guests had offered half-hearted excuses which nobody believed. One said he had a problem on the farm and had to rush home. Couldn't some. Sorry.

Another said he was into business and was about to sign a big deal. Had to stay with it. Couldn't come. Sorry. Another said he was going fishing. Couldn't put it off. Weather might change. Another said he had a family to attend to. Had to go home. Couldn't come. Nobody was willing to accept the invitation to come to the city to be present with the king to celebrate the wedding of his son.

The king got angry. He called out his troops and sent them to expel from his kingdom all those who had been invited to the wedding celebration. 'I never want to hear from those people again,' he said. 'I'm finished with them.'

He summoned his messengers and his heralds. 'It's about the wedding feast,' he said. 'I have changed the guest list. Go out into the highways and the byeways. Anyone you meet, invite them to the wedding. Tell them they are to be my guests at the great feast.' The heralds and the messengers went out to the four corners of the land. Anyone they chanced to meet on the way, they invited to the king's feast. All sorts came to the feast. And the Hall of Feasts was filled to capacity. And the king made them all welcome.

What does the invitation stand for ? What is the hidden meaning? When you look deeper, what do you see? What is it saying to us? How do you understand it?

We are invited into the action. We are invited into the presence of God, into friendship with God. But we have to make moves to accept the invitation. We have to say 'yes'. We have to go to some trouble. We have to work at getting there. Working to get there is about taking opportunities for doing good, moving towards God by following Jesus. Your invitation is to join the team, to walk with God, to be a follower of Jesus, a worker for the Kingdom. But the invitation has to get a response from you, has to be followed up with action.

The invitation could slip away from you. Don't let it gather dust. Take those opportunities. Do walk towards God. Do walk into his friendship. It's a festival of friendship that awaits you.

Call to Faith
We are invited to respond to God's invitation to come into the feast of God's friendship. We are invited to repond with deeds and actions. That is the way to come into the Feast of Friendship with God.

Call to Action
Play or sing a song /hymn with the theme of walking with God.
Parents, teachers and priests are the messengers who have invited us to the Feast of friendship with God. Thank them in words. Prepare a gift for them.

Twenty-Ninth Sunday

Gospel
A reading from the holy Gospel according to Matthew (22:15-21)
The Pharisees went off and made a plan to trap Jesus with questions. Then they sent to him some of their disciples and some members of Herod's party. 'Teacher,' they said, 'we know that you tell the truth. You teach the truth about God's will for man, without worrying what people think, because you pay no attention to a man's status. Tell us, then, what do you think? Is it against our Law to pay taxes to the Roman Emperor, or not?'

Jesus however was aware of their evil plan, and so he said, 'You hypocrites! Why are you trying to trap me? Show me the coin for paying the tax!'

They brought him the coin, and he asked them, 'Whose face and name are these?'

'The Emperor's,' they answered.

So Jesus said to them, 'Well, then, pay the Emperor what belongs to the Emperor, and pay God what belongs to God.'
This is the Gospel of the Lord

Overview

This gospel comes from a background of political accommodation between the Pharisees and the Herodians to achieve the grand aim, dear to both parties, of discrediting Jesus. When this opposition challenges Jesus to state his views on paying taxes to the emperor of Rome he doesn't allow them to lock him into a debate about taxes but points to the larger obligations we have to both Caesar and to God. We live in the secular world, yet we are God's children. Dues must be paid on both accounts.

For children it is best to talk about our obligations to our school, our home and also, very importantly, to God.

Focusing Experiences

Obigations we have at home. The chores around the house. The contribution we must make to family harmony. Obligations to our parents. Obligations to our brothers and sisters, to share with them, to encourage them, to defend them.

Obligations we have at school. Homework assignments. Listening and being attentive in class. Participating in sport, in school concerts, in projects. Caring for school grounds - being litter-conscious.

Obligations we have to our neighbourhood. To people in the neighbourhood. To facilities, like playgrounds and parks.

Exploring the Word of God

They thought they had him. The Herodians and the Pharisees were out to trap Jesus. They were out to show him up before the people. They were out to destroy his popularity. They were out to pull him down in the opinion of the people.

'Well, should the people pay taxes to Caesar or not? We want an answer,' they said. If Jesus said, 'Yes, pay taxes!' the local people would be offended because they were against paying taxes to the enemy. The high opinion they had of Jesus would be damaged. Jesus' popularity would be dented. If he said, 'No, don't pay taxes!' he would be breaking the law. They seemed to have him netted. 'Well,' they said, 'give us your answer.' They invited the people to crowd around to hear that answer.

'Have you a coin?' he said. They gave him a coin. He showed the coin to all the people. 'Whose picture is on this coin?' he asked, in a loud voice that carried to the end of the crowd. 'Caesar's,' they all said with one voice. 'Well then, give to the Roman Caesar what belongs to him.' And he raised a finger for silence. 'Give to God what belongs to God. Your obligations to God must never be forgotten or overlooked! Never!' The opposition were taken aback. The last thing in the world they wanted him to do was to talk about God. They wanted him to stop talking about God. That was their whole point. They believed they were the experts on God. And here he was being the voice of God to the people. The people thought he gave a marvellous answer and he gained new disciples. More importantly, they all crowded around to hear his advice on how they must meet their obligations to God. The opposition went off, furious that he had escaped from their little plot, and that he was talking in the name of God.

Call to Faith
We are called to give time and attention to home, to school and to our neighbourhood. We are also called, and this is a sacred obligation, to give time to God.

Call to Action
Review the time you give to God in Church, in school, in the parish, at home and elsewhere. Are you doing alright? Are you meeting your obligations?
Are there quiet times you could give to God, thinking times, maybe when you are alone?
Are there times you could read the Bible or a religious magazine?
Could you give some time to a worthy cause in the parish? Join the choir? Ask how you might help.
Sing a gentle song thanking God for his goodness and his love.

Thirtieth Sunday

Gospel
A reading from the holy Gospel according to Matthew(22:34-40)
When the Pharisees heard that Jesus had silenced the Sadducees, they came together, and one of them, a teacher of the Law, tried to trap him with a question. 'Teacher,' he asked, 'which is the greatest commandment of the Law?'

Jesus answered, 'Love the Lord your God with all your heart, with all your soul, and with all your mind. This is the greatest and the most important commandment. The second most important commandment is like it: love your neighbour as you love yourself. The whole Law of Moses and the teachings of the prophets depend on these two commandments.'
This is the Gospel of the Lord

Overview
They still still keep pursuing him. Jesus is not out of the woods yet. The opposition are still on his trail. This time they try to tangle him in a web about the relative importance of the many holy laws and statutes. It's a

minefield! They hope to show him up to be a man of straw. A man whose learned opinion can be shown to be only half true. No matter what he says, the opposite can be shown to be equally true. His acknowledged expertise on religious matters will take a tumble. He will be discredited before the people.

Jesus sweeps through all the laws and the statutes and gives priorities. Love God! he said. Love your neighbour! That's it, those are the priorities. No one, just no one, had said it that simply before. And it couldn't be faulted. It was brilliant. It must have come from someone who had the ear of God.

With children we should explore the inspired answer Jesus gave and leave the politics of the debate between him and the opposition to one side.

Focusing Experiences
The experience of love: What does it mean to be loved in the family? Any suggestions about what it means to be loved at home?

Cared for by parents
Defended by parents
Kissed by parents
Given pocket money by parents
Listened to by parents
Having your posters admired by parents .

Exploring the Word of God
'Love God, Love your neighbour,' says Jesus. Loving is about saying things in a certain way (with kindness, with patience, with good humour, with joy). Loving is about doing things in a certain way – being ready to help, to listen, to encourage, to praise. We want parents to be loving towards us in a million different ways. We have to love others in a million different ways as well. These ways of loving we learn from those who are loving towards us, like our parents and others close to us.

Loving is about feeling things in a certain way (feeling a little pain when others are hurt, feeling glad when others are glad, feeling a little sad when others are sad). Loving is about listening in a certain way (not just with the ears but with the heart).

We first try to understand the love we get from parents. Then we are able to give love because we know what we are talking about. It has happened to us.

Loving God is about listening to God in a certain way. With respect. With love. With openess. With confidence. Loving God is about feeling towards God in a certain way. Feeling a warmth towards God. Feeling a fondness towards God. Knowing that God is a friend. Feeling at home with God. Feeling right with God. Feeling we are loved by God. Feeling good with God. Feeling a loyalty towards God. Feeling happiness and contentment at the thought of God. Feeling a desire sometimes to be in God's company.

Love is about talking to God. Talking like we do at Mass. But also chatting as friends. Talking things over. Talking like people who know each other

Call to Faith
We are called to love God. We are called to love our neighbour.

Call to Action
Try to fill a page with your own experiences of love repeating the words:
    Love for me is ...
Find out something about the saints who loved God in a blissful way – the mystics.
Find out something about the system of those who consider that meditation is a way of expressing love for God.
Make out a list of practical ways of loving some of your neighbours.
Decorate Jesus' words: Love God. Love your neighbour.

Thirty-First Sunday

Gospel
A reading from the holy Gospel according to Matthew(23:1-12)
Then Jesus spoke to the crowds and to his disciples. 'The teachers of the Law and the Pharisees are the authorised interpreters of Moses' Law. So you must obey and follow everything they tell you to do; do not, however, imitate their actions, because they don't practice what they preach. They tie on to people's backs loads that are heavy and hard to carry, yet they aren't willing even to lift a finger to help them carry those loads. They do everything so that people will see them. Look at the straps with scripture verses on them which they wear on their foreheads and arms, and notice how large they are! Notice also how long are the tassels on their cloaks! They love the best places at feasts and the reserved seats in synagogues; they love to be greeted with respect in the market-places and to be called 'Teacher.' You must not be called 'Teacher,' because you are all brothers of one another and have only one teacher. And you must not call anyone here on earth 'Father,' because you have only the one

Father in heaven. Nor should you be called 'Leader,' because your one and only leader is the Messiah. The greatest one among you must be your servant. Whoever makes himself great will be humbled, and whoever humbles himself will be made great.'
This is the Gospel of the Lord

Overview
Matthew's gospel does not spare the Scribes and Pharisees. Their hypocrisy, their puffed-up importance, their external show all come under attack. When Matthew compiled and edited the words of Jesus, the Scribes and Pharisees had recently locked-out Jewish Christians from the Temple. So that may explain Matthew's powerful assembly of condemnatory material.

Self-seeking and worldly importance in Church leaders is condemned by Jesus. The Second Vatican Council faced up to this issue by affirming that service, not authority, is the key-role of Church leaders.

We have to encourage children to practise what they preach! This might be the most appropriate approach to this Sunday's gospel.

Focusing Experiences
What is hypocrisy?
- A child who praises the teacher to her face, but says horrible things about the teacher behind her back.
- A politician who leads a campaign against crime, but is in the pay of a crime syndicate.

We admire people who are 'on the level'. Who say what they mean. Who mean what they say. We admire people whose public statements are matched by their private actions.

We admire people who are sincere. We admire leaders who have a certain simplicity. We admire leaders who enjoy high office for the opportunity it gives them to help people. We are suspicious of leaders who enjoy their office for the glory it gives them. Glory seekers we call them.

Exploring the Word of God
Let's look at our own standards!
You say you should be treated fairly. Do you treat people fairly?
You say people should not give you a hard time. Do you ever give people a hard time?
You say you only did it for a laugh. Are you pleased or happy when people do it to you and say it was only done for a laugh?
You are angry when people steal from you. Did you ever steal from anyone? Are they entitled to be angry?
You say you have to have your say? Do you allow other people to have their say?

You say friends should be loyal to you. Are you loyal to your friends?
You say parents should do this or that for you. Do you do this or that for parents?
You say teachers should be this or that for you. Do you give teachers their rightful due in time, attention, generosity?
Are you a class leader? Are you a sports leader or captain? Are you one of a delegation? Does your job make you feel important? Make you feel good? Is that the most important thing for you? What about the opportunities the job gives you to help people, to make them feel good?

Call to Faith
We are called to be sincere. We are called to do the best we can. We are called to struggle with temptation. We are called to avoid pretending we are good to make a good impression, just to have people think well of us. We deserve to be called to order for using God's gift of goodness for our own selfish reasons.

Call to Action
Identify the opportunities young people of your age have for authority, influence or leadership: Class captain, Sports captain, Leader of a project, Captain of quiz team, Member of drama circle.
Have a discussion to identify the areas where people of your age might begin to feel better than everyone else, might begin to act 'bossy'.

Thirty-Second Sunday

Gospel
A reading from the holy Gospel according to Matthew (25:1-13)
At that time the kingdom of Heaven will be like this. Once there were ten girls who took their oil lamps and went to meet the bridegroom. Five of them were foolish and the other five were wise. The foolish ones took their lamps but did not take any extra oil with them, while the wise ones took containers full of oil for their lamps. The bridegroom was late in coming, so the girls began to nod and fall asleep.
   It was already midnight when the cry rang out, 'Here is the bridegroom! Come and meet him!' The ten girls woke up and trimmed their lamps. Then the foolish ones said to the wise ones, 'Let us have some of your oil, because our lamps are going out.''No, indeed,' the wise ones answered, 'there is not enough for you and for us. Go to the shop and buy some for yourselves.' So the foolish girls went off to buy some oil; and while they were gone, the bridegroom arrived. The five girls who were

ready went in with him to the wedding feast, and the door was closed.

Later the other girls arrived. 'Sir! Sir! Let us in!' they cried out. 'Certainly not! I don't know you!' the bridegroom answered.

And Jesus concluded, 'Be on your guard, then, because you do not know the day or the hour.'

This is the Gospel of the Lord.

Overview

We must one day pass through the gates of death to meet the Lord in judgement. We probably like to avoid the theme. We are not good at staring death in the face or preparing for death and judgement.

The judgement-day truth has been expressed down the ages in many ways, brilliantly and graphically in Michelangelo's Sistine Chapel or in Dante's *Inferno*. Today's people gloss over it. Probably we think the theological niceties of yesterday are a bit crude. Today heaven and hell have given way to appreciation of a relationship with God that is, in death and judgement, either deepened or else ruptured for good. Be that as it may, we still try to distance ourselves from death and its implications.

Today's gospel is a more distanced expression of the theme of death and judgement than that on the walls of the Sistine Chapel. The theme is dressed in the story of the bridesmaids who were late for the wedding. If we go, in death, unprepared for our judgement we are in deep trouble.

Children can deal easily enough with 'when you die stories' because death is not so immediate for them. (It terrifies us!) They should find this gospel story fascinating.

Focusing Experiences
Death.
Grief.
Funerals.
Graveyards.
Tombstones.
Graves.
Coffins.
Wakes.
People lying in state.
Funeral parlours.

Exploring the Word of God
When we die we face the judgement. Jesus shines the light of judgement on us. The good people are separated from the evil people. The sheep are separated from the goats. The good join God and his angels. The evil join the devil and a life of separation from God. For some it is a judgement

that brings bliss. For others a judgement that brings desolation. For some the outcome is happiness, for others it is pain and loneliness.

The good and the bad. Heaven or hell. Light or darkness. Music or hideous noise. Laughter or gnashing of teeth. Sunshine or prison. Death and judgement will reveal all.

Jesus tells a story about the importance of preparing for the day of our judgement. Get it right, he says, or face the consequences for ever.

These maidens were preparing to give a bridegroom a big welcome. They were going to meet him down the road and accompany him in a torchlight procession to the Banqueting Hall where he was, naturally, to be the guest of honour. It was a lovely idea. Something special. Add splendour to the occasion.

There were ten maidens. Each of them had a lamp. Five of the maidens had their lamps filled with oil. The other five didn't have oil in their lamps. This five, who didn't seem to be able to make proper preparations, planned to buy oil and be ready in time. They figured there was plenty of time. No problem. And there were plenty of shops and stores around. No need to fuss! No rush! No hassle!

Scouts were out to scan the road. But there was no sign of the bridegroom and his party. He was due at about six. Six o'clock came and went, and still no sign. Hours passed. It was clear that the bridgroom was delayed. People began to get drowsy and fell asleep.

A shout went up at midnight, 'The bridegroom is coming!' Everyone rushed for the doors. The five wise maidens lit their lamps and hurried out to be part of the action. They were at their posts in plenty of time. They were there ahead of time. The five foolish maidens went into a real flap. They had no oil. They wouldn't be able to accompany the bridegroom into the Wedding Feast. What were they to do? They hurried down to where the other maidens were assembling and begged them for oil. 'No way!' said the wise maidens. 'There mightn't be enough for you and for us. You'll have to buy. Try the stores.' The foolish maidens ran helter skelter for the stores. But of course the stores were all locked up for the night. They peered through the window of one place and saw lights in a backroom. They tried to rouse the shopkeeper. But no luck. They got no answer. The light went out and there was silence. Their knocking was in vain. They made their way back to their posts but the procession of honour for the Bridegroom had already gone. The procession was already inside in the Banqueting Hall. The music had begun, the food was being served, the door was firmly shut. In those days they didn't just shut a door at a wedding. A great plank was dropped into place across the length of the door. It was shut for the duration. The foolish maidens began to shout out, 'Lord, Lord, open the door for us.' But he repied, 'I do not know you.' And they were left outside. Never got in! Never!

So, Jesus said, when he finished his story, 'Prepare in life for the judgement in death. Be ready. Don't let yourself be shut out of heaven. Prepare!'

Call to Faith
We are called to follow Jesus. We are called to follow Jesus in a way that will prepare us for heaven and our eternal life of friendship with God.

Call to Action
Write down what you think heaven is like.
Write down what you think hell is like.
Imagine your own Judgement. Draw a picture.
Write slogans to remind people to prepare for Judgement Day.
Pray for the dead (ask the group to arrange an informal liturgy).
Pray to the dead.

Thirty-Third Sunday

Gospel
A reading from the holy Gospel according to Matthew (25:14-30)
Jesus spoke this parable to his disciples: 'At that time the Kingdom of Heaven will be like this. Once there was a man who was about to go on a journey; he called his servants and put them in charge of his property. He gave to each one according to his ability: to one he gave five thousand gold coins, to another he gave two thousand, and to another he gave one thousand. Then he left on his journey.

'The servant who had received five thousand coins went at once and invested his money and earned another five thousand.In the same way the servant who had received two thousand coins earned another two thousand. But the servant who had received one thousand coins went off, dug a hole in the ground, and hid his master's money.

'After a long time, the master of those servants came back and settled accounts with them. The servant who had received five thousand coins came in and handed over the other five thousand. 'You gave me five thousand coins, Sir,' he said. 'Look! Here are another five thousand that I have earned.' 'Well done, you good and faithful servant!' said the master. 'You have been faithful in managing small amounts, so I will put you in charge of large amounts. Come on in and share my happiness!' 'Then the servant who had been given two thousand coins came in and said,

'You gave me two thousand coins, Sir. Look! Here are another two thousand that I have earned.' 'Well done, you good and faithful servant!' said his master. 'You have been faithful in managing small amounts, so I will put you in charge of large amounts. Come on in and share my happiness!' 'Then the servant who had received one thousand coins came in and said, 'Sir, I know you are a hard man; you reap harvests where you did not sow, and you gather crops where you did not scatter seed. I was afraid, so I went off and hid your money in the ground. Look! Here is what belongs to you.' 'You bad and lazy servant!' his master said. 'You knew, did you, that I reap harvest where I did not sow, and gather crops where I did not scatter seed? Well, then, you should have deposited my money in the bank, and I would have received it all back with interest when I returned. Now, take the money away from him and give it to the one who has ten thousand coins. For to every person who has something, even more will be given, and he will have more than enough; but the person who has nothing, even the little he has will be taken away from him. As for this useless servant – throw him outside in the darkness, there he will cry and grind his teeth.'
This is the Gospel of the Lord.

Overview
This is a gospel story built around investment and profit. God is presented as a capitalist! He invests in us and he expects a return. We are entrusted with responsibilities. We have to render an account. We have to face the moment of audit. It's a really lovely story and the children will respond to it. For children the kernel must be that we are given the gift of love by God. We are called to share that love around and about. It's a serious obligation. We have to give a report on our efforts.

Focusing Experiences
Have you ever been trusted to take care of a pet when a friend is away on vacation?
Has your family ever been trusted with a tent, a summer house, a cottage which neighbours feel you will leave in good shape after you?
Parents ever trust you to make sure things are ok while they are out?
Lawyers are sometimes entrusted with a case which they conduct to the best of their ability in court.
Priests are entrusted with responsibility for bringing Jesus to the people of God.
Teachers are entrusted with responsibility for the education of their class.
Parents are entrusted with the care and love of their children.
We are all entrusted to take care of our health. We are given responsibility for whatever gifts or talents we have.

Exploring the Word of God

We are entrusted by God with the gift of love. We are entrusted by God to make that gift active. We are entrusted by God to make that gift work for our good and the good of all.

Jesus told this story about gold coins that were entrusted in the hope of a good return:

There was this great man man who had a big farm, with plenty of cattle grazing in his fields, and lovely horses in a large meadow before a big house. He had outhouses on the farm bigger than bungalows, and no shortage of money.

He called his three top servants to a big meeting. 'Look,' he said, 'I am going to be away for a while. I have to tour the world for a few years. When I am away in foreign parts I want each one of you to look after a part of my wealth.'

He called the first servant. 'Take these five thousand gold coins,' he said. 'Make them work for me when I am away. Do the best you can for me with the part of my fortune entrusted to you. Good man!'

He called the second servant. 'Here,' he said, 'are two thousand gold coinsfor you. Make them work for me when I am away. Do the best you can for me. Good luck!'

He called his third servant. He gave him one thousand gold coins. 'Here you are,' he said, 'take it. Make it work for me. Do the best you can. I wish you well in this responsibility.'

And the great man went off around the world.

The servant who got the five thousand coins immediately set to work. He loaned a few thousand to some solid citizens, banked a few thousand and invested what was left. Later he bought some land and sold sites for houses. He bought and sold cattle. He had lots of schemes and ideas. Everything seemed to work for him. He managed the money well. Did nothing foolish. The money he got from the great man began to grow.

The second servant who was given the two thousand coins wasted no time either. He set about dealing and trading, buying and selling. He was in and out of banks and market places doing business. People admired his energy and enthusiasm and his skill in trading. His money began to grow too. It had to. He was very good at what he was doing.

The third servant who got the one thousand – that was a different story. He carefully wrapped the coins he was given in a piece of cloth, then put them into a bag and buried them in the ground. He smoothed out the ground and left the coins buried there.

The great man finished travelling around the world and came home. The first thing he did was to call the servants to another big meeting. 'Well,' he said, 'how did it go? How did you get on? I entrused each one of you with a share of my fortune. Give me your reports!' The servant

---

who got five thousand showed his results. He had managed to double what he was given. 'Marvellous,' said the great man. 'Well done! Excellent! First class. You couldn't have done any better.'

It was the same for the second. He had doubled what he was given. He was praised up and down. Highly complimented.

The servant who got the one thousand told how he had buried what he was given in the ground. Yes, buried and covered. No one could touch it. He didn't do anything with it. No one did. He left it there. He couldn't think of anything worthwhile and anyway he was afraid to use it. Now he held up the bundle of coins for the great man to see. They were as new and as fresh as the day he got them. Unused. Untouched.

The great man looked at him very sharply and couldn't believe what he was hearing. The great man began to jump up and down in a rage. He banged the table with his fist. He shouted, and threw his arms into the air. He got very red and agitated. When he calmed down he said to the servant, 'That's just not good enough. I gave you a responsibility and what did you do? Nothing!! What efforts did you make? None! You hid your money in the ground. You let it lie there. What good was that to me? This is a very big disappointment. A very big disappointment. I have to say to you that I do feel let down. You wasted the money. It could have been working for me. You didn't show any energy, any interest. We'll have to do something about this. I could never think of giving you responsibility again.' He took the money from that man and gave it to the servant with the five thousand. 'I can trust you. I know you'll make it work for me. You won't let me down.'

He turned to the servant who buried the coins in the ground. 'Out!' he said, 'You're finished here. You're gone! Your dead wood! You had your chance. You blew it.'

And that servant walked away feeling very sorry for himself.

Call to Faith
We receive God's love. We are called to pass it on. We are given the responsibility of sharing it around, of making it grow.

Call to Action
Write a poem about the servant who hid the talent.
How are you spreading God's love around? Do a report on yourself for God.
Any ideas for improving the quality of life, love, worshsip in the parish or in the neighbourhood.
To what cause or activities in the parish or in the neighbourhood would you be willing to devote more time?
Do something active for a friend in hospital.
Write a letter (or make a colourful postcard) to a friend.

Our Lord Jesus Christ, Universal King

Last Sunday in Ordinary Time

Gospel
A reading from the holy Gospel according to Matthew (25: 31-46)
Jesus said to his disciples, 'When the Son of Man comes as King and all the angels with him, he will sit on his royal throne, and the people of all the nations will be gathered before him. Then he will divide then into two groups, just as a shepherd separates the sheep from the goats. He will put the righteous people on his right and the others on his left. Then the King will say to the people on his right, 'Come, you that are blessed by my Father! Come and possess the Kingdom which has been prepared for you ever since the creation of the world. I was hungry and you fed me, thirsty and you gave me a drink; I was a stranger and you received me in your homes, naked and you clothed me; I was sick and you took care of me, in prison and you visited me.'

'The righteous will then answer him, 'When, Lord, did we ever see you hungry and feed you, or thirsty and give you a drink? When did we ever see you a stranger and welcome you in our homes, or naked and clothe you?' The King will reply, 'I tell you, whenever you did this for one of the least important of these brothers of mine, you did it for me.'

'Then he will say to those on his left, 'Away from me, you that are under God's curse! Away to the eternal fire which has been prepared for the Devil and his angels! I was hungry but you would not feed me, thirsty and you would not give me a drink; I was a stranger but you would not welcome me in your homes, naked but you would not clothe me; I was sick and in prison but you would not take care of me.'

Then they will answer him, 'When, Lord did we ever see you hungry or thirsty or a stranger or naked or sick or in prison, and would not help you?' The King will reply, 'I tell you, whenever you refused to help one of these least important ones, you refused to help me.' These, then, will be sent off to eternal punishment, but the righteous will go to eternal life.'
This is the Gospel of the Lord.

Overview
The twist about this gospel is that while Jesus is feted as king he is really an anti-king. He doesn't fit the popular model of king. He is quite the opposite. Power, prestige, wealth, ambition are not part of his trappings. With Jesus, we have to coin a new meaning for kingship. He is king of love. King of our hearts. King of justice. King of fellowship. King of peace. King of dreams and hopes.

Children have vivid imaginations. They have no problem transferring people into a new costume, a new set or cirumstances, or of moving out of stereo-types. Jesus is not a king of land and territories, not a king of marching armies, but a king of ideas and hopes. A king of dreams, a king who leads us gently and quietly to love each other and cherish each other, to build a new world for God.

The story of heaven and hell, sheep and goats, right and left, glory or damnation, should not be told to the children like a news item, to frighten. It should be told to the imagination. It's a story with a deep truth. A truth to ponder and reflect on. A pointer. A nugget of wisdom to remind us of a great reality.

Focusing Experiences

We use the word king to refer to kings who lived in their great castles and ruled kingdoms and had servants to wait on them: King of England, King of France, King of the Aztecs. Remember any more?

We also use the word king to signify greatness, or a special skill in some area. It's a compliment, a special title, a tribute, a word of praise: king of musicians, king of cowboys, king of explorers, king of the animals, king of pop stars, king of peace, king of ideas.

Exploring the Word of God

Jesus told this story about the Lord King of Heaven and Judgement Day. The king of heaven is in the great throne room which stretches further than the eye can see. Magnificence everywhere. Colours of every kind and hue, silver and gold light stretching and contracting, flowing and ebbing, to fill your mind with wonder and delight. High ceilings with sparkling glass chandeliers. Walls decorated with the most wonderful pictures and drawings. And soft music everywhere to please the heart.

The King is sitting on his throne. He is accompanied by the angels and saints. Millions of people stand before him. From every continent. From every state. From every town. From every village.

It is time for their judgement. There is silence. A very deep silence. A look of judgement from the king is directed at every single one. People wait, and hear their judgement in the quietness of their heart. Each person walks to join either the condemned or to join the elect of God. The elect to the right, the condemned to the left. Those who join the elect walk to the place of glory with a quick firm step, shoulders held high and joy in their eyes. Those who join the condemned, droop their shoulders, hang their heads and look deeply troubled.

The elect are gathered on the king's right. The condemned are huddled on his left. He turns to those on his right. 'Welcome, a thousand welcomes,' he says. 'You are blessed and blessed again. And this is your

---

glory, this is your credit; when I was hungry you gave me food. When I was thirsty you gave me drink. When I was a stranger you made me feel welcome. Take your place in the kingdom of glory prepared for you.'

The king turns to those on his left. 'Go away from me. Go away from me. There is a curse upon you. And this is your shame, this is your downfall: when I was hungry you gave me no food. When I was thirsty you gave me no drink. When I was a stranger you never made me feel welcome! Take you place with the devils in the place of darkness and damnation.'

There is a cry from the condemned and they plead with the king. 'Lord, Lord,' they say, 'We never saw you hungry or thirsty. We never met you as a stranger and ignored you. We would never do such a thing to you. There must be a mistake.'

The king answers. 'I tell you solemnly,' he says 'as long as you did it to one of these, the least of my people, you did it to me!'

The elect are led in a joyous procession into their glory. The others, the condemned, are directed to the place of darkness to begin eternal damnation.

Call to Faith
We are called to be people of action, of welcome, of consideration, of sensitivity. We are all called to be brothers and sisters. We are called to look out for each other. We are called to see Christ in the poor and in the weak and in the helpless.

We are called to follow Jesus our King. The king of the beggars. The king of the down and outs. The king of the weak. The king of the handicapped. The king of the disabled. The king of the poor.

Call to Action
How can we help the poor? Ask the Vincent de Paul Society for advice. Invite one of the brothers or sisters to meet the group.

How can we help the imprisoned? Ask a prison chaplain. They will be able to suggest useful ways.

Sing songs of compassion like 'Jesus my brother'.

Have a procession, carrying placards with slogans like: Jesus, King of our hearts; Jesus, King of Justice; Jesus, King of Peace.

The Feast of All Saints

Gospel
A reading from the holy Gospel according to Matthew (5: 1-10)
Jesus saw the crowds and went up a hill, where he sat down. His disciples gathered around him, and he began to teach them:
Happy are those who mourn;
God will comfort them!
Happy are those who are humble;
they will receive what God has promised!
Happy are those whose greatest desire is to do what God requires;
God will satisfy them fully!
Happy are those who are merciful to others;
God will be merciful to them!
Happy are the pure in heart;
they will see God!
They are those who work for peace;
God will call them his children!
Happy are those who are persecuted because they do what God requires;
the Kingdom of heaven belongs to them!
This is the Gospel of the Lord.

Overview
Saints are the recognised official heroes among the people of God. Their deeds have won them this recognition. Their names have been given to churches, their portraits carved in marble or bronze, their deeds often remembered in stained glass windows or Church murals. On this day we honour them. We honour them with words.

Children like to honour with words, but also with processions and placards, with speeches, with song. All Saints day is a day for children to remember Church heroes and also their own personal Christian heroes whose kindness they have experienced, whose love has touched them. On this day their names should be posted up and honoured.

Focusing Experiences
Have a memories recall. Review the events of the past year. What memories stand out? What events made a big impression on you?
Review the experiences you had with people during the past year. What people stand out? What happened that made a big impression on you - an experience of forgiveness, of support, of friendship, of understanding, of shared excitement, of discovery?

Exploring the word of God

Here is the saints' coat- of- arms, their motto, their song, their theme. It's taken from the Bible. These ideals for living, cherished by the saints, are called the Beatitudes:

1. Be small before God; God will make you great!
2. Go to God in your sadness; God will take away your tears.
3. Show heart to others; God will show heart to you.
4. Let others see you as you are; God will let you see the glory of God.
5. Bring peace to your friends: God will bring peace to you.
6. Work for God, even if it costs you pain and trouble; God will work for you today, tomorrow and always.

Call to Faith

We are called to honour the names of the great saints. We are called to honour those who blazed a trail of goodness in the world in which they lived. We are called to be inspired by the heroic deeds of these great people.

We are also called to honour the quiet saints, our own personal heroes, people we appreciate, people who brought some little gift of love or kindness into our lives.

Call to Action

Explore the lives of the saints. Pick the name of a saint who worked in an area that impresses you – worked with lepers, worked where an epidemic broke out, worked in a city area, worked in prisons. Do a small research project. Conclude the project by writing a short tribute of praise to the saint whose work you have come to know and admire.

Have a procession of tribute to the saints whose names have some association with the group. Highlight the name of a favourite saints on a placard with supporting words describing their essential contribution to the people of God. Walk in this procession of honour and tribute.

Post the names of everyday 'saints' who have touched your lives in some way with saintly qualities, in a sealed envelope, which is placed on the altar to be honoured with prayers and blessings.

Assumption of the Blessed Virgin Mary

Gospel

A reading from the holy Gospel according to Luke (1: 39-56)

Soon afterwards, Mary got ready and hurried off to a town in the hill-country of Judea. She went into Zechariah's house and greeted Elizabeth. When Elizabeth heard Mary's greeting, the baby moved within her. Elizabeth was filled with the Holy Spirit and said in a loud voice, 'You are the most blessed of all women, and blessed is the child you will bear! Why should this great thing happen to me, that my Lord's mother comes to visit me? For assoon as I heard your greeting, the baby within me jumped with gladness. How happy you are to believe that the Lord's message to you will come true!' Mary said:

'My heart praises the Lord,

my soul is glad because of God my Saviour,

for he has remembered me, his lowly servant!

From now on, all people will call me happy,

because of the great thing the mighty God has done for me.

His name is holy;

from one generation to another

he shows mercy to those who honour him.

He has stretched out his mighty arm

and scattered the proud with all their plans.

He has brought down mighty kings from their thrones,

and lifted up the lowly.

He has filled the hungry with good things,

and sent the rich away with empty hands.

He has kept the promise he made to our ancestors,

and has come to the help of his servant Israel.

He has remembered to show mercy to Abraham

and to all his descendants forever!'

Mary stayed about three months with Elizabeth and then went back home.

This is the Gospel of the Lord.

Overview

The wisdom of many generations of Christians has recorded a preference for honouring Mary with processions, floral tributes, hymn singing, and banners carried in her honour.

The Assumption expresses the Church's recognition of the high place Mary has won in the heart of God. On this feastday the children should be encouraged to express with minds, hearts, feet and hands their tribute to Mary.

Focusing Experiences
Ask the group to think about the Mary, Mother of Jesus. What do they remember about her? What elements do they remember of her story in Bethlehem, in Nazareth, at the wedding feast, at the foot of the cross? What pieces of art work of Mary do they remember? What have they seen on TV about shrines dedicated to Mary – Lourdes, Knock?
How is Mary honoured in your local Church?
What prayers are said to honour Mary or invoke her help?

Exploring the Word of God
Mary was expecting a baby. She made a journey to Judah to visit her cousin, Elizabeth, who was also expecting a baby. As soon as Mary walked in the door of her cousin's house, Elizabeth went into a sort of ecstasy and began to prophesy about Mary like a prophet of God would. She proclaimed that Mary was chosen by God, that Mary was blessed among the women of the world. She said that Mary brought honour and glory to God. She said that the child in Mary's womb was the Saviour of the world. It was an amazing outpouring of prophetic words.

Mary, deeply moved by what Elizabeth said, broke into a hymn of praise to God.

When she finished, they both knew that they had experienced the hand of God in their lives. And they were very quiet and still for some time.

Call to Faith
We are called to honour Mary. We are called to acknowledge her as the mother of God. We are called to pay her a tribute of praise, respect and devotion.

Call to Action
Arrange a special procession in honour of Mary. Prepare banners, flowers and decorations. Sing Marian hymns and say prayers to Mary.
Recite together some of the age-old prayers to Mary.
Recite the Rosary together to experience that old family tradition of saying the rosary each night in the home.